The Constitution of
The State of Oregon:
A Quick Reference Guide

Bootblack Budget Books
Copyright 2018 ©
ISBN-13: 978-1721093212
ISBN-10: 1721093214

Contents:

Article III: Distribution of Powers – Page 80

Section 1. Separation of Powers

Section 2. Budgetary Control Over Executive and Administrative Officers and Agencies

Section 3. Joint Legislative Committee to Allocate Emergency Fund Appropriations and to Authorize Expenditures Beyond Budgetary Limits

Section 4. Senate, Confirmation of Executive Appointments

Article IV: Legislative Branch – Page 83

Article V: Executive Branch – Page 103

Article VII: Judicial Branch – Page 113

Article VIII: Education and School Lands – Page 119

Article IX: Finance – Page 123

Section 1. Assessment and Taxation; Uniform Rules; Uniformity of Operation of Laws

Section 1a. Poll or Head Tax; Declaration of Emergency in Tax Laws

Section 1b. Ships Exempt from Taxation Until 1935

Section 1c. Financing Redevelopment and Urban Renewal Projects

Section 2. Legislature to Provide Revenue to Pay Current State Expenses and Interest

Section 3. Tax Imposed Only by Law; Statement of Purpose

Section 3a. Use of Revenue from Taxes on Motor Vehicle Use and Fuel; Legislative Review of Allocation of Taxes Between Vehicle Classes

Section 3b. Rate of Levy on Oil or Natural Gas; Exception

Section 4. Appropriation Necessary for Withdrawal From Treasury

Section 5. Publication of Accounts

Section 6. Deficiency of Funds; Tax Levy to Pay

Section 7. Appropriation Laws not to Contain Provisions on other Subjects

Section 8. Stationery for Use of State

Section 9. Taxation of Certain Benefits Prohibited

Section 10. Retirement Plan Contributions by Governmental Employees

Section 11. Retirement Plan Rate of Return Contract Guarantee Prohibited

Section 12. Retirement not to be Increased by Unused Sick Leave

Section 13. Retirement Plan Restriction Severability

Section 14. Revenue Estimate; Retention of Excess Corporate Tax Revenue in General Fund for Public Education Funding; Return of other Excess Revenue to Taxpayers; Legislative Increase in Estimate

Section 15. Prohibition on Tax, Fee or other Assessment Upon Transfer of Interest in Real Property; Exception

Article X-A: Catastrophic Disasters – Page 133

Section 1. Definitions; Declaration of Catastrophic Disaster; Convening of Legislative Assembly

Section 2. Additional Powers of Governor; use of General Fund Moneys and Lottery Funds

Section 3. Procedural Requirements for Legislative Assembly

Section 4. Additional Powers of Legislative Assembly

Section 5. Participation in Session of Legislative Assembly by Electronic Or Other Means

Section 6. Termination of Operation of this Article; Extension by Legislative Assembly; Transition Provisions; Limitation on Power of Governor to Invoke this Article

Article XI: Corporations and
Internal Improvements – Page 140

Section 1. Prohibition of State Banks

Section 2. Formation of Corporations; Municipal Charters; Intoxicating Liquor Regulation

Section 2a. Merger of Adjoining Municipalities; County-City Consolidation

Section 3. Liability of Stockholders

Section 4. Compensation for Property Taken by Corporation

Section 5. Restriction of Municipal Powers in Acts of Incorporation

Section 6. State not to Be Stockholder in Company; Exceptions; Inapplicability to Public Universities

Section 7. Credit of State not to be Loaned; Limitation Upon Power of Contracting Debts

Section 8. State not to Assume Debts of Counties, Towns or Other Corporations

Section 9. Limitations on Powers of County or City to Assist Corporations

Section 10. County Debt Limitation

Section 11. Property Tax Limitations on Assessed Value And Rate of Tax; Exceptions

Section 11b. Property Tax Categories; Limitation on Categories; Exceptions

Section 11c. Limits in Addition to Other Tax Limits

Section 11d. Effect of Section 11b on Exemptions And Assessments

Section 11e. Severability of Sections 11b, 11c And 11d

Section 11k. Limitation on Applicability of Section 11 (8) Voting Requirements to Elections on Measures Held in May or November of Any Year

Section 11l. Limitation on Applicability of Sections 11 And 11b on Bonded Indebtedness to Finance Capital Costs

Section 12. People's Utility Districts

Section 13. Interests of Employees When Operation of Transportation System Assumed by Public Body

Section 14. Metropolitan Service District Charter

Section 15. Funding of Programs Imposed Upon Local Governments; Exceptions

Article XI-A: Farm and Home
Loans to Veterans – Page 172

ARTICLE XI-B: State Payment of Irrigation and Drainage District Interest – Page 176

Repealed

ARTICLE XI-C: World War Veterans State Aid Sinking Fund – Page 177

Repealed

Article XI-E: State Reforestation – Page 180

Section 1. State Empowered to Lend Credit for Forest Rehabilitation and Reforestation; Bonds; Taxation

Article XI-F(1): Higher Education Building Projects – Page 181

Section 1. State Empowered to Lend Credit for Higher Education Building Projects

Section 2. Limitation on Authorization to Incur Indebtedness

Section 3. Sources of Revenue

Section 4. Bonds

Section 5. Legislation to Effectuate Article

Article XI-F(2): Veterans Bonus – Page 183

Section 1. State Empowered to Lend Credit to Pay Veterans Bonus; Issuance of Bonds

Section 2. Definitions

Section 3. Amount of Bonus

Section 4. Survivors of Certain Deceased Veterans Entitled to Maximum Amount

Section 5. Certain Persons not Eligible

Section 6. Order of Distribution Among Survivors

Section 7. Bonus Not Saleable or Assignable; Bonus Free From Creditors Claims and State Taxes

Section 8. Administration of Article; Rules and Regulations

Section 9. Applications

Section 10. Furnishing Forms; Printing, Office Supplies and Equipment; Employees; Payment of Expenses

Article XI-G: Higher Education Institutions and Activities; Community Colleges – Page 189

Section 1. State Empowered to Lend Credit for Financing Higher Education Institutions and Activities, and Community Colleges

Section 2. Bonds

Section 3. Sources of Revenue

Article XI-H: Pollution Control – Page 191

Section 1. State Empowered to Lend Credit for Financing Pollution Control Facilities or Related Activities

Section 2. Only Facilities 70 Percent Self-Supporting and Self-Liquidating Authorized; Exceptions

Section 3. Authority of Public Bodies to Receive Funds

Section 4. Sources of Revenue

Section 5. Bonds

Section 6. Legislation to Effectuate Article

Article XI-I(2): Multifamily Housing
for Elderly and Disabled – Page 195

Section 1. State Empowered to Lend Credit for Multifamily Housing for Elderly and Disabled Persons

Section 2. Sources of Revenue

Section 3. Bonds

Section 4. Legislation to Effectuate Article

Article XI-K: Guarantee of Bonded Indebtedness of Education Districts – Page 198

Section 1. State Empowered to Guarantee Bonded Indebtedness of Education Districts

Section 2. State Empowered to Lend Credit for State Guarantee of Bonded Indebtedness of Education Districts

Section 3. Repayment by Education Districts

Section 4. Sources of Revenue

Section 5. Bonds

Section 6. Legislation to Effectuate Article

Article XI-M: Seismic Rehabilitation of Public Education Buildings – Page 204

Section 1. State Empowered to Lend Credit for Seismic Rehabilitation of Public Education Buildings; Bonds

Section 2. Sources of Repayment

Section 3. Refunding Bonds

Section 4. Legislation to Effectuate Article

Section 5. Relationship to Conflicting Provisions of Constitution

Article XI-N: Seismic Rehabilitation of Emergency Services Buildings – Page 206

Section 1. State Empowered to Lend Credit for Seismic Rehabilitation of Emergency Services Buildings; Bonds

Section 2. Sources of Repayment

Section 3. Refunding Bonds

Section 4. Legislation to Effectuate Article

Section 5. Relationship to Conflicting Provisions of Constitution

Article XI-O: Pension Liabilities – Page 209

Section 1. State Empowered to Lend Credit for Pension Liabilities

Section 2. Refunding Obligations

Section 3. Legislation to Effectuate Article

Section 4. Relationship to Conflicting Provisions of Constitution

39

Article XI-P: School District Capital Costs – Page 210

Section 1. State Empowered to Lend Credit for Grants or Loans to School Districts to Finance Capital Costs; General Obligation Bond Proceeds as Matching Funds

Section 2. Sources of Repayment

Section 3. Refunding Bonds

Section 4. School Capital Matching Fund

Section 5. "Capital Costs" Defined

Section 6. Legislation to Effectuate Article

Section 7. Relationship to Conflicting Provision of Constitution

Article XI-Q: Real or Personal Property Owned or Operated by State – Page 213

Section 1. State Empowered to Lend Credit for Real or Personal Property to be Owned or Operated by State; Refinancing Authority

Section 2. Limit on Indebtedness; General Obligation of State

Section 3. Legislation to Effectuate Article

Section 4. Relationship to Conflicting Provisions of Constitution

Article XII: State Printing – Page 215

Section 1. State printing; State Printer

Article XIII: Salaries – Page 216

Repealed

Article XIV: Seat of Government – Page 217

Section 1. Seat of Government

Section 2. Erection of State House Prior to 1865

44

Article XV: Miscellaneous – Page 218

Section 9. When Elective Office Becomes Vacant

Section 10. The Oregon Property Protection Act of 2000

Section 11. Home Care Commission

Article XVI: Boundaries – Page 241

Section 1. State Boundaries

Article XVII: Amendments and Revisions – Page 242

Section 1. Method of Amending Constitution

Section 2. Method of Revising Constitution

48

Article XVIII: Schedule – Page 245

Section 1. Election to Accept or Reject Constitution

Section 2. Questions Submitted to Voters

Section 3. Majority of Votes Required to Accept or Reject Constitution

Section 4. Vote on Certain Sections of Constitution

Section 5. Apportionment of Senators and Representatives

Section 6. Election Under Constitution; Organization of State

Section 7. Former Laws Continued in Force

Section 8. Officers to Continue in Office

Section 9. Crimes Against Territory

Section 10. Saving Existing Rights and Liabilities

Section 11. Judicial Districts

PREAMBLE:

We the people of the State of Oregon to the end that Justice be established, order maintained, and liberty perpetuated, do ordain this Constitution

ARTICLE I: BILL OF RIGHTS

Section 1. Natural Rights Inherent in People

We declare that all men, when they form a social compact are equal in right: that all power is inherent in the people, and all free governments are founded on their authority, and instituted for their peace, safety, and happiness; and they have at all times a right to alter, reform, or abolish the government in such manner as they may think proper.

Section 2. Freedom of Worship

All men shall be secure in the Natural right, to worship Almighty God according to the dictates of their own consciences.

Section 3. Freedom of Religious Opinion

No law shall in any case whatever control the free exercise, and enjoyment of religeous [sic] opinions, or interfere with the rights of conscience.

Section 4. No religious Qualification for Office

No religious test shall be required as a qualification for any office of trust or profit.

Section 5. No Money to be Appropriated for Religion

No money shall be drawn from the Treasury for the benefit of any religeous [sic], or theological institution, nor shall any money be appropriated for the payment of any religeous [sic] services in either house of the Legislative Assembly.

Section 6. No Religious Test for Witnesses or Jurors

No person shall be rendered incompetent as a witness, or juror in consequence of his opinions on matters of religeon [sic]; nor be questioned in any Court of Justice touching his religeous [sic] belief to affect the weight of his testimony.

Section 7. Manner of Administering Oath or Affirmation

The mode of administering an oath, or affirmation shall be such as may be most consistent with, and binding upon the conscience of the person to whom such oath or affirmation may be administered.

Section 8. Freedom of Speech and Press

No law shall be passed restraining the free expression of opinion, or restricting the right to speak, write, or print freely on any subject whatever; but every person shall be responsible for the abuse of this right.

Section 9. Unreasonable Searches or Seizures

No law shall violate the right of the people to be secure in their persons, houses, papers, and effects, against unreasonable search, or seizure; and no warrant shall issue but upon probable cause, supported by oath, or affirmation, and particularly describing the place to be searched, and the person or thing to be seized.

Section 10. Administration of Justice

No court shall be secret, but justice shall be administered, openly and without purchase, completely and without delay, and every man shall have remedy by due course of law for injury done him in his person, property, or reputation.

Section 11. Rights of Accused in Criminal Prosecution

In all criminal prosecutions, the accused shall have the right to public trial by an impartial jury in the county in which the offense shall have been committed; to be heard by himself and counsel;

to demand the nature and cause of the accusation against him, and to have a copy thereof; to meet the witnesses face to face, and to have compulsory process for obtaining witnesses in his favor; provided, however, that any accused person, in other than capital cases, and with the consent of the trial judge, may elect to waive trial by jury and consent to be tried by the judge of the court alone, such election to be in writing; provided, however, that in the circuit court ten members of the jury may render a verdict of guilty or not guilty, save and except a verdict of guilty of first degree murder, which shall be found only by a unanimous verdict, and not otherwise; provided further, that the existing laws and constitutional provisions relative to criminal prosecutions shall be continued and remain in effect as to all prosecutions for crimes committed before the taking effect of this amendment.

Section 12. Double Jeopardy; Compulsory Self-Incrimination

No person shall be put in jeopardy twice for the same offence [sic], nor be compelled in any criminal prosecution to testify against himself.

Section 13. Treatment of Arrested or Confined Persons

No person arrested, or confined in jail, shall be treated with unnecessary rigor.

Section 14. Bailable Offenses

Offences [sic], except murder, and treason, shall be bailable by sufficient sureties. Murder or treason, shall not be bailable, when the proof is evident, or the presumption strong

Section 15. Foundation Principles of Criminal Law

Laws for the punishment of crime shall be founded on these principles: protection of society, personal responsibility, accountability for one's actions and reformation.

Section 16. Excessive Bail and Fines; Cruel and Unusual Punishments; Power of Jury in Criminal Case

Excessive bail shall not be required, nor excessive fines imposed. Cruel and unusual punishments shall not be inflicted, but all penalties shall be proportioned to the offense.

In all criminal cases whatever, the jury shall have the right to determine the law, and the facts under the direction of the Court as to the law, and the right of new trial, as in civil cases.

Section 17. Jury Trial In Civil Cases

In all civil cases the right of Trial by Jury shall remain inviolate.

Section 18. Private Property or Services Taken for Public Use

Private property shall not be taken for public use, nor the particular services of any man be demanded, without just compensation; nor except in the case of the state, without such compensation first assessed and tendered; provided, that the use of all roads, ways and waterways necessary to promote the transportation of the raw products of mine or farm or forest or water for beneficial use or drainage is necessary to the development and welfare of the state and is declared a public use.

Section 19. Imprisonment for Debt

There shall be no imprisonment for debt, except in case of fraud or absconding debtors.

Section 20. Equality of Privileges and Immunities of Citizens

No law shall be passed granting to any citizen or class of citizens privileges, or immunities, which, upon the same terms, shall not equally belong to all citizens.

Section 21. Ex-Post Facto Laws; Laws Impairing Contracts; Laws Depending On Authorization In Order To Take Effect; Laws Submitted To Electors

No ex-post facto law, or law impairing the obligation of contracts shall ever be passed, nor shall any law be passed, the taking effect of which shall be made to depend upon any authority, except as provided in this Constitution; provided, that laws locating the Capitol of the State, locating County Seats, and submitting town, and corporate acts, and other local, and Special laws may take effect, or not, upon a vote of the electors interested.

Section 22. Suspension of Operation of Laws

The operation of the laws shall never be suspended, except by the Authority of the Legislative Assembly.

Section 23. Habeas Corpus

The privilege of the writ of habeas corpus shall not be suspended unless in case of rebellion, or invasion the public safety require it.

Section 24. Treason

Treason against the State shall consist only in levying war against it, or adhering to its enemies, giving them aid or comfort.

No person shall be convicted of treason unless on the testimony of two witnesses to the same overt act, or confession in open Court.

Section 25. Corruption of Blood or Forfeiture of Estate

No conviction shall work corruption of blood, or forfeiture of estate.

Section 26. Assemblages of People; Instruction of Representatives; Application to Legislature

No law shall be passed restraining any of the inhabitants of the State from assembling together in a peaceable manner to consult for their common good; nor from instructing their Representatives; nor from applying to the Legislature for redress of greviances [sic].

Section 27. Right to Bear Arms; Military Subordinate to Civil Power

The people shall have the right to bear arms for the defence [sic] of themselves, and the State, but the Military shall be kept in strict subordination to the civil power.

Section 28. Quartering Soldiers

No soldier shall, in time of peace, be quartered in any house, without the consent of the owner, nor in time of war, except in the manner prescribed by law.

Section 29. Titles of Nobility; Hereditary Distinctions

No law shall be passed granting any title of Nobility, or conferring hereditary distinctions.

Section 30. Emigration

No law shall be passed prohibiting emigration from the State.

Section 31. Rights of Aliens; Immigration to State

Repealed

Section 32. Taxes and Duties; Uniformity of Taxation

No tax or duty shall be imposed without the consent of the people or their representatives in the Legislative Assembly; and all taxation shall be uniform on the same class of subjects within the territorial limits of the authority levying the tax.

Section 33. Enumeration of Rights not Exclusive

This enumeration of rights, and privileges shall not be construed to impair or deny others retained by the people.

Section 34. Slavery or Involuntary Servitude

There shall be neither slavery, nor involuntary servitude in the State, otherwise than as a punishment for crime, whereof the party shall have been duly convicted.

Section 35. Restrictions on Rights of Certain Persons

Repealed

Section 36. Liquor Prohibition

Repealed

Section 36. Capital Punishment Abolished

Repealed

Section 36a. Prohibition of Importation of Liquors

Repealed

Section 37. Penalty for Murder in First Degree

Repealed

Section 38. Laws Abrogated by Amendment Abolishing Death
Penalty Revived

Repealed

Section 39. Sale of Liquor by Individual Glass

The State shall have power to license private clubs, fraternal
organizations, veterans' organizations, railroad corporations
operating interstate trains and commercial establishments where
food is cooked and served, for the purpose of selling alcoholic
liquor by the individual glass at retail, for consumption on the
premises, including mixed drinks and cocktails, compounded or
mixed on the premises only. The Legislative Assembly shall
provide in such detail as it shall deem advisable for carrying out
and administering the provisions of this amendment and shall
provide adequate safeguards to carry out the original intent and
purpose of the Oregon Liquor Control Act, including the
promotion of temperance in the use and consumption of
alcoholic beverages, encourage the use and consumption of
lighter beverages and aid in the establishment of Oregon
industry. This power is subject to the following:

(1) The provisions of this amendment shall take effect and be in
operation sixty (60) days after the approval and adoption by the
people of Oregon; provided, however, the right of a local option
election exists in the counties and in any incorporated city or
town containing a population of at least five hundred (500). The
Legislative Assembly shall prescribe a means and a procedure by
which the voters of any county or incorporated city or town as
limited above in any county, may through a local option election
determine whether to prohibit or permit such power, and such
procedure shall specifically include that whenever fifteen per cent
(15%) of the registered voters of any county in the state or of
any incorporated city or town as limited above, in any county in
the state, shall file a petition requesting an election in this
matter, the question shall be voted upon at the next regular
November biennial election, provided said petition is filed not less

than sixty (60) days before the day of election.

(2) Legislation relating to this matter shall operate uniformly throughout the state and all individuals shall be treated equally; and all provisions shall be liberally construed for the accomplishment of these purposes.

Section 40. Penalty for Aggravated Murder

Notwithstanding sections 15 and 16 of this Article, the penalty for aggravated murder as defined by law shall be death upon unanimous affirmative jury findings as provided by law and otherwise shall be life imprisonment with minimum sentence as provided by law.

Section 41. Work and Training for Corrections Institution Inmates; Work Programs; Limitations; Duties of Corrections Director

(1) Whereas the people of the state of Oregon find and declare that inmates who are confined in corrections institutions should work as hard as the taxpayers who provide for their upkeep; and whereas the people also find and declare that inmates confined within corrections institutions must be fully engaged in productive activity if they are to successfully re-enter society with practical skills and a viable work ethic; now, therefore, the people declare:

(2) All inmates of state corrections institutions shall be actively engaged full-time in work or on-the-job training. The work or on-the-job training programs shall be established and overseen by the corrections director, who shall ensure that such programs are cost-effective and are designed to develop inmate motivation, work capabilities and cooperation. Such programs may include boot camp prison programs. Education may be provided to inmates as part of work or on-the-job training so long as each inmate is engaged at least half-time in hands-on training or work activity.

(3) Each inmate shall begin full-time work or on-the-job training immediately upon admission to a corrections institution, allowing for a short time for administrative intake and processing. The specific quantity of hours per day to be spent in work or on-the-job training shall be determined by the corrections director, but the overall time spent in work or training shall be full-time. However, no inmate has a legally enforceable right to a job or to otherwise participate in work, on-the-job training or educational programs or to compensation for work or labor performed while an inmate of any state, county or city corrections facility or institution. The corrections director may reduce or exempt participation in work or training programs by those inmates deemed by corrections officials as physically or mentally disabled, or as too dangerous to society to engage in such programs.

(4) There shall be sufficient work and training programs to ensure that every eligible inmate is productively involved in one or more programs. Where an inmate is drug and alcohol addicted so as to prevent the inmate from effectively participating in work or training programs, corrections officials shall provide appropriate drug or alcohol treatment.

(5) The intent of the people is that taxpayer-supported institutions and programs shall be free to benefit from inmate work. Prison work programs shall be designed and carried out so as to achieve savings in government operations, so as to achieve a net profit in private sector activities or so as to benefit the community.

(6) The provisions of this section are mandatory for all state corrections institutions. The provisions of this section are permissive for county or city corrections facilities. No law, ordinance or charter shall prevent or restrict a county or city governing body from implementing all or part of the provisions of this section. Compensation, if any, shall be determined and established by the governing body of the county or city which chooses to engage in prison work programs, and the governing body may choose to adopt any power or exemption allowed in this section.

(7) The corrections director shall contact public and private enterprises in this state and seek proposals to use inmate work. The corrections director may: (a) install and equip plants in any state corrections institution, or any other location, for the employment or training of any of the inmates therein; or (b) purchase, acquire, install, maintain and operate materials, machinery and appliances necessary to the conduct and operation of such plants. The corrections director shall use every effort to enter into contracts or agreements with private business concerns or government agencies to accomplish the production or marketing of products or services produced or performed by inmates. The corrections director may carry out the director's powers and duties under this section by delegation to others.

(8) Compensation, if any, for inmates who engage in prison work programs shall be determined and established by the corrections director. Such compensation shall not be subject to existing public or private sector minimum or prevailing wage laws, except where required to comply with federal law. Inmate compensation from enterprises entering into agreements with the state shall be exempt from unemployment compensation taxes to the extent allowed under federal law. Inmate injury or disease attributable to any inmate work shall be covered by a corrections system inmate injury fund rather than the workers compensation law. Except as otherwise required by federal law to permit transportation in interstate commerce of goods, wares or merchandise manufactured, produced or mined, wholly or in part by inmates or except as otherwise required by state law, any compensation earned through prison work programs shall only be used for the following purposes: (a) reimbursement for all or a portion of the costs of the inmate's rehabilitation, housing, health care, and living costs; (b) restitution or compensation to the victims of the particular inmate's crime; (c) restitution or compensation to the victims of crime generally through a fund designed for that purpose; (d) financial support for immediate family of the inmate outside the corrections institution; and (e) payment of fines, court costs, and applicable taxes.

(9) All income generated from prison work programs shall be kept separate from general fund accounts and shall only be used for implementing, maintaining and developing prison work programs. Prison industry work programs shall be exempt from statutory competitive bid and purchase requirements. Expenditures for prison work programs shall be exempt from the legislative appropriations process to the extent the programs rely on income sources other than state taxes and fees. Where state taxes or fees are the source of capital or operating expenditures, the appropriations shall be made by the legislative assembly. The state programs shall be run in a businesslike fashion and shall be subject to regulation by the corrections director. Expenditures from income generated by state prison work programs must be approved by the corrections director. Agreements with private enterprise as to state prison work programs must be approved by the corrections director. The corrections director shall make all state records available for public scrutiny and the records shall be subject to audit by the Secretary of State.

(10) Prison work products or services shall be available to any public agency and to any private enterprise of any state, any nation or any American Indian or Alaskan Native tribe without restriction imposed by any state or local law, ordinance or regulation as to competition with other public or private sector enterprises. The products and services of corrections work programs shall be provided on such terms as are set by the corrections director. To the extent determined possible by the corrections director, the corrections director shall avoid establishing or expanding for-profit prison work programs that produce goods or services offered for sale in the private sector if the establishment or expansion would displace or significantly reduce preexisting private enterprise. To the extent determined possible by the corrections director, the corrections director shall avoid establishing or expanding prison work programs if the establishment or expansion would displace or significantly reduce government or nonprofit programs that employ persons with developmental disabilities. However, the decision to establish, maintain, expand, reduce or terminate any prison work program remains in the sole discretion of the corrections director.

(11) Inmate work shall be used as much as possible to help operate the corrections institutions themselves, to support other government operations and to support community charitable organizations. This work includes, but is not limited to, institutional food production; maintenance and repair of buildings, grounds, and equipment; office support services, including printing; prison clothing production and maintenance; prison medical services; training other inmates; agricultural and forestry work, especially in parks and public forest lands; and environmental clean-up projects. Every state agency shall cooperate with the corrections director in establishing inmate work programs.

(12) As used throughout this section, unless the context requires otherwise: "full-time" means the equivalent of at least forty hours per seven day week, specifically including time spent by inmates as required by the Department of Corrections, while the inmate is participating in work or on-the-job training, to provide for the safety and security of the public, correctional staff and inmates; "corrections director" means the person in charge of the state corrections system.

(13) This section is self-implementing and supersedes all existing inconsistent statutes. This section shall become effective April 1, 1995. If any part of this section or its application to any person or circumstance is held to be invalid for any reason, then the remaining parts or applications to any persons or circumstances shall not be affected but shall remain in full force and effect.

Section 42. (Declared Void) Rights of Victim in Criminal Prosecutions and Juvenile Court Delinquency Proceedings

(1) To preserve and protect the right of crime victims to justice, to ensure crime victims a meaningful role in the criminal and juvenile justice systems, to accord crime victims due dignity and respect and to ensure that criminal and juvenile court delinquency proceedings are conducted to seek the truth as to the defendant's innocence or guilt, and also to ensure that a fair balance is struck between the rights of crime victims and the rights of criminal defendants in the course and conduct of criminal and juvenile court delinquency proceedings, the following rights are hereby granted to victims in all prosecutions for crimes and in juvenile court delinquency proceedings:

(a) The right to be present at and, upon specific request, to be informed in advance of any critical stage of the proceedings held in open court when the defendant will be present, and to be heard at the pretrial release hearing and the sentencing or juvenile court delinquency disposition;

(b) The right, upon request, to obtain information about the conviction, sentence, imprisonment, criminal history and future release from physical custody of the criminal defendant or convicted criminal and equivalent information regarding the alleged youth offender or youth offender;

(c) The right to refuse an interview, deposition or other discovery request by the criminal defendant or other person acting on behalf of the criminal defendant provided, however, that nothing in this paragraph shall restrict any other constitutional right of the defendant to discovery against the state;

(d) The right to receive prompt restitution from the convicted criminal who caused the victim's loss or injury;

(e) The right to have a copy of a transcript of any court proceeding in open court, if one is otherwise prepared;

(f) The right to be consulted, upon request, regarding plea negotiations involving any violent felony; and

(g) The right to be informed of these rights as soon as practicable.

(2) This section applies to all criminal and juvenile court delinquency proceedings pending or commenced on or after the effective date of this section. Nothing in this section reduces a criminal defendant's rights under the Constitution of the United States. Except as otherwise specifically provided, this section supersedes any conflicting section of this Constitution. Nothing in this section is intended to create any cause of action for compensation or damages nor may this section be used to invalidate an accusatory instrument, conviction or adjudication or otherwise terminate any criminal or juvenile delinquency proceedings at any point after the case is commenced or on appeal. Except as otherwise provided in subsections (3) and (4) of this section, nothing in this section may be used to invalidate a ruling of a court or to suspend any criminal or juvenile delinquency proceedings at any point after the case is commenced.

(3)(a) Every victim described in paragraph (c) of subsection

(6) of this section shall have remedy by due course of law for violation of a right established in this section.

(b) A victim may assert a claim for a right established in this section in a pending case, by a mandamus proceeding if no case is pending or as otherwise provided by law.

(c) The Legislative Assembly may provide by law for further effectuation of the provisions of this subsection, including authorization for expedited and interlocutory consideration of claims for relief and the establishment of reasonable limitations on the time allowed for bringing such claims.

(d) No claim for a right established in this section shall suspend a criminal or juvenile delinquency proceeding if such a suspension would violate a right of a criminal defendant guaranteed by this Constitution or the Constitution of the United States.

(4) Upon the victim's request, the prosecuting attorney, in the attorney's discretion, may assert and enforce a right established in this section.

(5) Upon the filing by the prosecuting attorney of an affidavit setting forth cause, a court shall suspend the rights established in this section in any case involving organized crime or victims who are minors.

(6) As used in this section:

(a) "Convicted criminal" includes a youth offender in juvenile court delinquency proceedings.

(b) "Criminal defendant" includes an alleged youth offender in juvenile court delinquency proceedings.

(c) "Victim" means any person determined by the prosecuting attorney or the court to have suffered direct financial, psychological or physical harm as a result of a crime and, in the case of a victim who is a minor, the legal guardian of the minor.

(d) "Violent felony" means a felony in which there was actual or threatened serious physical injury to a victim or a felony sexual offense.

(7) In the event that no person has been determined to be a victim of the crime, the people of Oregon, represented by the prosecuting attorney, are considered to be the victims. In no event is it intended that the criminal defendant be considered the victim.

Section 43. Rights of Victim and Public to Protection From Accused Person During Criminal Proceedings; Denial of Pretrial Release

(1) To ensure that a fair balance is struck between the rights of crime victims and the rights of criminal defendants in the course and conduct of criminal proceedings, the following rights are hereby granted to victims in all prosecutions for crimes:

(a) The right to be reasonably protected from the criminal defendant or the convicted criminal throughout the criminal justice process and from the alleged youth offender or youth offender throughout the juvenile delinquency proceedings.

(b) The right to have decisions by the court regarding the pretrial release of a criminal defendant based upon the principle of reasonable protection of the victim and the public, as well as the likelihood that the criminal defendant will appear for trial. Murder, aggravated murder and treason shall not be bailable when the proof is evident or the presumption strong that the person is guilty. Other violent felonies shall not be bailable when a court has determined there is probable cause to believe the criminal defendant committed the crime, and the court finds, by clear and convincing evidence, that there is danger of physical injury or sexual victimization to the victim or members of the public by the criminal defendant while on release.

(2) This section applies to proceedings pending or commenced on or after the effective date of this section. Nothing in this section abridges any right of the criminal defendant guaranteed by the Constitution of the United States, including the rights to be represented by counsel, have counsel appointed if indigent, testify, present witnesses, cross-examine witnesses or present information at the release hearing. Nothing in this section creates any cause of action for compensation or damages nor may this section be used to invalidate an accusatory instrument, conviction or adjudication or otherwise terminate any criminal or juvenile delinquency proceeding at any point after the case is commenced or on appeal. Except as otherwise provided in paragraph (b) of subsection (4) of this section and in subsection (5) of this section, nothing in this section may be used to invalidate a ruling of a court or to suspend any criminal or juvenile delinquency proceedings at any point after the case is commenced. Except as otherwise specifically provided, this section supersedes any conflicting section of this Constitution.

(3) As used in this section:

(a) "Victim" means any person determined by the prosecuting attorney or the court to have suffered direct financial, psychological or physical harm as a result of a crime and, in the case of a victim who is a minor, the legal guardian of the minor. **(b)** "Violent felony" means a felony in which there was actual or threatened serious physical injury to a victim or a felony sexual offense.

(4)(a) The prosecuting attorney is the party authorized to assert the rights of the public established by this section.

(b) Upon the victim's request, the prosecuting attorney, in the attorney's discretion, may assert and enforce a right established in this section.

(5)(a) Every victim described in paragraph (a) of subsection (3) of this section shall have remedy by due course of law for violation of a right established in this section.

(b) A victim may assert a claim for a right established in this section in a pending case, by a mandamus proceeding if no case is pending or as otherwise provided by law.

(c) The Legislative Assembly may provide by law for further effectuation of the provisions of this subsection, including authorization for expedited and interlocutory consideration of claims for relief and the establishment of reasonable limitations on the time allowed for bringing such claims.

(d) No claim for a right established in this section shall suspend a criminal or juvenile delinquency proceeding if such a suspension would violate a right of a criminal defendant or alleged youth offender guaranteed by this Constitution or the Constitution of the United States.

(6) In the event that no person has been determined to be a victim of the crime, the people of Oregon, represented by the prosecuting attorney, are considered to be the victims. In no event is it intended that the criminal defendant be considered the victim.

Section 44. Term of Imprisonment Imposed by Court to be Fully Served; Exceptions

(1)(a) A term of imprisonment imposed by a judge in open court may not be set aside or otherwise not carried out, except as authorized by the sentencing court or through the subsequent exercise of:

(A) The power of the Governor to grant reprieves, commutations and pardons; or

(B) Judicial authority to grant appellate or post-conviction relief.

(b) No law shall limit a court's authority to sentence a criminal defendant consecutively for crimes against different victims.

(2) This section applies to all offenses committed on or after the effective date of this section. Nothing in this section reduces a criminal defendant's rights under the Constitution of the United States. Except as otherwise specifically provided, this section supersedes any conflicting section of this Constitution. Nothing in this section creates any cause of action for compensation or damages nor may this section be used to invalidate an accusatory instrument, ruling of a court, conviction or adjudication or otherwise suspend or terminate any criminal or juvenile delinquency proceedings at any point after the case is commenced or on appeal.

(3) As used in this section, "victim" means any person determined by the prosecuting attorney to have suffered direct financial, psychological or physical harm as a result of a crime and, in the case of a victim who is a minor, the legal guardian of the minor. In the event no person has been determined to be a victim of the crime, the people of Oregon, represented by the prosecuting attorney, are considered to be the victims. In no event is it intended that the criminal defendant be considered the victim.

Section 45. Person Convicted of Certain Crimes not Eligible to Serve as Juror on Grand Jury or Trial Jury in Criminal Case

(1) In all grand juries and in all prosecutions for crimes tried to a jury, the jury shall be composed of persons who have not been convicted:

(a) Of a felony or served a felony sentence within the 15 years immediately preceding the date the persons are required to report for jury duty; or

(b) Of a misdemeanor involving violence or dishonesty or served a sentence for a misdemeanor involving violence or dishonesty within the five years immediately preceding the date the persons are required to report for jury duty.

(2) This section applies to all criminal proceedings pending or commenced on or after the effective date of this section, except a criminal proceeding in which a jury has been impaneled and sworn on the effective date of this section. Nothing in this section reduces a criminal defendant's rights under the Constitution of the United States. Except as otherwise specifically provided, this section supersedes any conflicting section of this Constitution. Nothing in this section is intended to create any cause of action for compensation or damages nor may this section be used to disqualify a jury, invalidate an accusatory instrument, ruling of a court, conviction or adjudication or otherwise suspend or terminate any criminal proceeding at any point after a jury is impaneled and sworn or on appeal.

Section 46. Prohibition on Denial or Abridgment of Rights on Account of Sex

(1) Equality of rights under the law shall not be denied or abridged by the State of Oregon or by any political subdivision in this state on account of sex.

(2) The Legislative Assembly shall have the power to enforce, by appropriate legislation, the provisions of this section.

(3) Nothing in this section shall diminish a right otherwise available to persons under section 20 of this Article or any other provision of this Constitution.

ARTICLE II: SUFFRAGE AND ELECTIONS

Section 1. Elections Free

All elections shall be free and equal.

Section 2. Qualifications of Electors

(1) Every citizen of the United States is entitled to vote in all elections not otherwise provided for by this Constitution if such citizen:

(a) Is 18 years of age or older;

(b) Has resided in this state during the six months immediately preceding the election, except that provision may be made by law to permit a person who has resided in this state less than 30 days immediately preceding the election, but who is otherwise qualified under this subsection, to vote in the election for candidates for nomination or election for President or Vice President of the United States or elector of President and Vice President of the United States; and

(c) Is registered not less than 20 calendar days immediately preceding any election in the manner provided by law.

(2) Provision may be made by law to require that persons who vote upon questions of levying special taxes or issuing public bonds shall be taxpayers.

Section 3. Rights of Certain Electors

A person suffering from a mental handicap is entitled to the full rights of an elector, if otherwise qualified, unless the person has been adjudicated incompetent to vote as provided by law. The privilege of an elector, upon conviction of any crime which is punishable by imprisonment in the penitentiary, shall be forfeited, unless otherwise provided by law.

Section 4. Residence

For the purpose of voting, no person shall be deemed to have gained, or lost a residence, by reason of his presence, or absence while employed in the service of the United States, or of this State; nor while engaged in the navigation of the waters of this State, or of the United States, or of the high seas; nor while a student of any Seminary of Learning; nor while kept at any alms house, or other assylum [sic], at public expence [sic]; nor while confined in any public prison.

Section 5. Soldiers, Seamen and Marines; Residence; Right to Vote

No soldier, seaman, or marine in the Army, or Navy of the United States, or of their allies, shall be deemed to have acquired a residence in the state, in consequence of having been stationed within the same; nor shall any such soldier, seaman, or marine have the right to vote.

Section 6. Right of Suffrage for Certain Persons

Repealed

Section 7. Bribery at Elections

Every person shall be disqualified from holding office, during the term for which he may have been elected, who shall have given, or offered a bribe, threat, or reward to procure his election.

Section 8. Regulation of Elections

The Legislative Assembly shall enact laws to support the privilege of free suffrage, prescribing the manner of regulating, and conducting elections, and prohibiting under adequate penalties, all undue influence therein, from power, bribery, tumult, and other improper conduct.

Section 9. Penalty for Dueling

Every person who shall give, or accept a challenge to fight a duel, or who shall knowingly carry to another person such challenge, or who shall agree to go out of the State to fight a duel, shall be ineligible to any office of trust, or profit.

Section 10. Lucrative Offices; Holding Other Offices Forbidden

No person holding a lucrative office, or appointment under the United States, or under this State, shall be eligible to a seat in the Legislative Assembly; nor shall any person hold more than one lucrative office at the same time, except as in this Constition [sic] expressly permitted; Provided, that Officers in the Militia, to which there is attached no annual salary, and the Office of Post Master, where the compensation does not exceed One Hundred Dollars per annum, shall not be deemed lucrative.

Section 11. When Collector or Holder of Public Moneys Ineligible to Office

No person who may hereafter be a collector, or holder of public moneys, shall be eligible to any office of trust or profit, until he shall have accounted for, and paid over according to law, all sums for which he may be liable.

Section 12. Temporary Appointments to Office

In all cases, in which it is provided that an office shall not be filled by the same person, more than a certain number of years continuously, an appointment pro tempore shall not be reckoned a part of that term.

Section 13. Privileges of Electors

In all cases, except treason, felony, and breach of the peace, electors shall be free from arrest in going to elections, during their attendance there, and in returning from the same; and no elector shall be obliged to do duty in the Militia on any day of election, except in time of war, or public danger.

Section 14. Time of Holding Elections and Assuming Duties of Office

The regular general biennial election in Oregon for the year A. D. 1910 and thereafter shall be held on the first Tuesday after the first Monday in November. All officers except the Governor, elected for a six year term in 1904 or for a four year term in 1906 or for a two year term in 1908 shall continue to hold their respective offices until the first Monday in January, 1911; and all officers, except the Governor elected at any regular general biennial election after the adoption of this amendment shall assume the duties of their respective offices on the first Monday in January following such election. All laws pertaining to the nomination of candidates, registration of voters and all other things incident to the holding of the regular biennial election shall be enforced and be effected the same number of days before the first Tuesday after the first Monday in November that they have heretofore been before the first Monday in June biennially, except as may hereafter be provided by law.

Section 14a. Time of Holding Elections in Incorporated Cities And Towns

Incorporated cities and towns shall hold their nominating and regular elections for their several elective officers at the same time that the primary and general biennial elections for State and county officers are held, and the election precincts and officers shall be the same for all elections held at the same time. All provisions of the charters and ordinances of incorporated cities and towns pertaining to the holding of elections shall continue in full force and effect except so far as they relate to the time of holding such elections. Every officer who, at the time of the adoption of this amendment, is the duly qualified incumbent of an elective office of an incorporated city or town shall hold his office for the term for which he was elected and until his successor is elected and qualified. The Legislature, and cities and towns, shall enact such supplementary legislation as may be necessary to carry the provisions of this amendment into effect.

Section 15. Method of voting in legislature

In all elections by the Legislative Assembly, or by either branch thereof, votes shall be given openly or viva voce, and not by ballot, forever; and in all elections by the people, votes shall be given openly, or viva voce, until the Legislative Assembly shall otherwise direct.

Section 16. Election by Plurality; Proportional Representation

In all elections authorized by this constitution until otherwise provided by law, the person or persons receiving the highest number of votes shall be declared elected, but provision may be made by law for elections by equal proportional representation of all the voters for every office which is filled by the election of two or more persons whose official duties, rights and powers are equal and concurrent. Every qualified elector resident in his precinct and registered as may be required by law, may vote for one person under the title for each office. Provision may be made by law for the voter's direct or indirect expression of his first, second or additional choices among the candidates for any office. For an office which is filled by the election of one person it may be required by law that the person elected shall be the final choice of a majority of the electors voting for candidates for that office. These principles may be applied by law to nominations by political parties and organizations.

Section 17. Place of Voting

All qualified electors shall vote in the election precinct in the County where they may reside, for County Officers, and in any County in the State for State Officers, or in any County of a Congressional District in which such electors may reside, for Members of Congress.

Section 18. Recall; Meaning of Words "The Legislative Assembly Shall Provide."

(1) Every public officer in Oregon is subject, as herein provided, to recall by the electors of the state or of the electoral district from which the public officer is elected.

(2) Fifteen per cent, but not more, of the number of electors who voted for Governor in the officer's electoral district at the most recent election at which a candidate for Governor was elected to a full term, may be required to file their petition demanding the officer's recall by the people.

(3) They shall set forth in the petition the reasons for the demand.

(4) If the public officer offers to resign, the resignation shall be accepted and take effect on the day it is offered, and the vacancy shall be filled as may be provided by law. If the public officer does not resign within five days after the petition is filed, a special election shall be ordered to be held within 35 days in the electoral district to determine whether the people will recall the officer.

(5) On the ballot at the election shall be printed in not more than 200 words the reasons for demanding the recall of the officer as set forth in the recall petition, and, in not more than 200 words, the officer's justification of the officer's course in office. The officer shall continue to perform the duties of office until the result of the special election is officially declared. If an officer is recalled from any public office the vacancy shall be filled immediately in the manner provided by law for filling a vacancy in that office arising from any other cause.

(6) The recall petition shall be filed with the officer with whom a petition for nomination to such office should be filed, and the same officer shall order the special election when it is required. No such petition shall be circulated against any officer until the officer has actually held the office six months, save and except that it may be filed against a senator or representative in the legislative assembly at any time after five days from the beginning of the first session after the election of the senator or representative.

(7) After one such petition and special election, no further recall petition shall be filed against the same officer during the term for which the officer was elected unless such further petitioners first pay into the public treasury which has paid such special election expenses, the whole amount of its expenses for the preceding special election.

(8) Such additional legislation as may aid the operation of this section shall be provided by the legislative assembly, including provision for payment by the public treasury of the reasonable special election campaign expenses of such officer. But the words, "the legislative assembly shall provide," or any similar or equivalent words in this constitution or any amendment thereto, shall not be construed to grant to the legislative assembly any exclusive power of lawmaking nor in any way to limit the initiative and referendum powers reserved by the people.

Section 22. Political Campaign Contribution Limitations

Section (1) For purposes of campaigning for an elected public office, a candidate may use or direct only contributions which originate from individuals who at the time of their donation were residents of the electoral district of the public office sought by the candidate, unless the contribution consists of volunteer time, information provided to the candidate, or funding provided by federal, state, or local government for purposes of campaigning for an elected public office.

Section (2) Where more than ten percent (10%) of a candidate's total campaign funding is in violation of Section (1), and the candidate is subsequently elected, the elected official shall forfeit the office and shall not hold a subsequent elected public office for a period equal to twice the tenure of the office sought. Where more than ten percent (10%) of a candidate's total campaign funding is in violation of Section (1) and the candidate is not elected, the unelected candidate shall not hold a subsequent elected public office for a period equal to twice the tenure of the office sought.

Section (3) A qualified donor (an individual who is a resident within the electoral district of the office sought by the candidate) shall not contribute to a candidate's campaign any restricted contributions of Section (1) received from an unqualified donor for the purpose of contributing to a candidate's campaign for elected public office. An unqualified donor (an entity which is not an individual and who is not a resident of the electoral district of the office sought by the candidate) shall not give any restricted contributions of Section (1) to a qualified donor for the purpose of contributing to a candidate's campaign for elected public office.

Section (4) A violation of Section (3) shall be an unclassified felony.

Section 23. Approval by More Than Majority Required for Certain Measures Submitted to People

(1) Any measure that includes any proposed requirement for more than a majority of votes cast by the electorate to approve any change in law or government action shall become effective only if approved by at least the same percentage of voters specified in the proposed voting requirement.
(2) For the purposes of this section, "measure" includes all initiatives and all measures referred to the voters by the Legislative Assembly.

(3) The requirements of this section apply to all measures presented to the voters at the November 3, 1998 election and thereafter.

(4) The purpose of this section is to prevent greater-than-majority voting requirements from being imposed by only a majority of the voters.

Section 24. Death of candidate prior to election

When any vacancy occurs in the nomination of a candidate for elective public office in this state, and the vacancy is due to the death of the candidate, the Legislative Assembly may provide by law that:

(1) The regularly scheduled election for that public office may be postponed;

(2) The public office may be filled at a subsequent election; and

(3) Votes cast for candidates for the public office at the regularly scheduled election may not be considered.

ARTICLE III: DISTRIBUTION OF POWERS

Section 1. Separation of Powers

The powers of the Government shall be divided into three separate branches, the Legislative, the Executive, including the administrative, and the Judicial; and no person charged with official duties under one of these branches, shall exercise any of the functions of another, except as in this Constitution expressly provided.

Section 2. Budgetary Control Over Executive and Administrative Officers and Agencies

The Legislative Assembly shall have power to establish an agency to exercise budgetary control over all executive and administrative state officers, departments, boards, commissions and agencies of the State Government.

Section 3. Joint Legislative Committee to Allocate Emergency Fund Appropriations and to Authorize Expenditures Beyond Budgetary Limits

(1) The Legislative Assembly is authorized to establish by law a joint committee composed of members of both houses of the Legislative Assembly, the membership to be as fixed by law, which committee may exercise, during the interim between sessions of the Legislative Assembly, such of the following powers as may be conferred upon it by law:

(a) Where an emergency exists, to allocate to any state agency, out of any emergency fund that may be appropriated to the committee for that purpose, additional funds beyond the amount appropriated to the agency by the Legislative Assembly, or funds to carry on an activity required by law for which an appropriation was not made.

(b) Where an emergency exists, to authorize any state agency to expend, from funds dedicated or continuously appropriated for the uses and purposes of the agency, sums in excess of the amount of the budget of the agency as approved in accordance with law.

(c) In the case of a new activity coming into existence at such a time as to preclude the possibility of submitting a budget to the Legislative Assembly for approval, to approve, or revise and approve, a budget of the money appropriated for such new activity.

(d) Where an emergency exists, to revise or amend the budgets of state agencies to the extent of authorizing transfers between expenditure classifications within the budget of an agency.

(2) The Legislative Assembly shall prescribe by law what shall constitute an emergency for the purposes of this section.

(3) As used in this section, "state agency" means any elected or appointed officer, board, commission, department, institution, branch or other agency of the state government.

(4) The term of members of the joint committee established pursuant to this section shall run from the adjournment of one odd-numbered year regular session to the organization of the next odd-numbered year regular session. No member of a committee shall cease to be such member solely by reason of the expiration of his term of office as a member of the Legislative Assembly.

Section 4. Senate Confirmation of Executive Appointments

(1) The Legislative Assembly in the manner provided by law may require that all appointments and re-appointments to state public office made by the Governor shall be subject to confirmation by the Senate.

(2) The appointee shall not be eligible to serve until confirmed in the manner required by law and if not confirmed in that manner, shall not be eligible to serve in the public office.

(3) In addition to appointive offices, the provisions of this section shall apply to any state elective office when the Governor is authorized by law or this Constitution to fill any vacancy therein, except the office of judge of any court, United States Senator or Representative and a district, county or precinct office.

ARTICLE IV: LEGISLATIVE BRANCH

Section 1. Legislative Power; Initiative and Referendum

(1) The legislative power of the state, except for the initiative and referendum powers reserved to the people, is vested in a Legislative Assembly, consisting of a Senate and a House of Representatives.

(2)(a) The people reserve to themselves the initiative power, which is to propose laws and amendments to the Constitution and enact or reject them at an election independently of the Legislative Assembly.

(b) An initiative law may be proposed only by a petition signed by a number of qualified voters equal to six percent of the total number of votes cast for all candidates for Governor at the election at which a Governor was elected for a term of four years next preceding the filing of the petition.

(c) An initiative amendment to the Constitution may be proposed only by a petition signed by a number of qualified voters equal to eight percent of the total number of votes cast for all candidates for Governor at the election at which a Governor was elected for a term of four years next preceding the filing of the petition.

(d) An initiative petition shall include the full text of the proposed law or amendment to the Constitution. A proposed law or amendment to the Constitution shall embrace one subject only and matters properly connected therewith.

(e) An initiative petition shall be filed not less than four months before the election at which the proposed law or amendment to the Constitution is to be voted upon.

(3)(a) The people reserve to themselves the referendum power, which is to approve or reject at an election any Act, or part thereof, of the Legislative Assembly that does not become effective earlier than 90 days after the end of the session at which the Act is passed.

(b) A referendum on an Act or part thereof may be ordered by a petition signed by a number of qualified voters equal to four percent of the total number of votes cast for all candidates for Governor at the election at which a Governor was elected for a term of four years next preceding the filing of the petition. A referendum petition shall be filed not more than 90 days after the end of the session at which the Act is passed.

(c) A referendum on an Act may be ordered by the Legislative Assembly by law. Notwithstanding section 15b, Article V of this Constitution, bills ordering a referendum and bills on which a referendum is ordered are not subject to veto by the Governor.

(4)(a) Petitions or orders for the initiative or referendum shall be filed with the Secretary of State. The Legislative Assembly shall provide by law for the manner in which the Secretary of State shall determine whether a petition contains the required number of signatures of qualified voters. The Secretary of State shall complete the verification process within the 30-day period after the last day on which the petition may be filed as provided in paragraph (e) of subsection (2) or paragraph (b) of subsection (3) of this section.

(b) Initiative and referendum measures shall be submitted to the people as provided in this section and by law not inconsistent therewith.

(c) All elections on initiative and referendum measures shall be held at the regular general elections, unless otherwise ordered by the Legislative Assembly.

(d) Notwithstanding section 1, Article XVII of this Constitution, an initiative or referendum measure becomes effective 30 days after the day on which it is enacted or approved by a majority of the votes cast thereon. A referendum ordered by petition on a part of an Act does not delay the remainder of the Act from becoming effective.

(5) The initiative and referendum powers reserved to the people by subsections (2) and (3) of this section are further reserved to the qualified voters of each municipality and district as to all local, special and municipal legislation of every character in or for their municipality or district. The manner of exercising those powers shall be provided by general laws, but cities may provide the manner of exercising those powers as to their municipal legislation. In a city, not more than 15 percent of the qualified voters may be required to propose legislation by the initiative, and not more than 10 percent of the qualified voters may be required to order a referendum on legislation.

Section 1. Legislative Authority Vested in Assembly; Initiative and Referendum; Style of Bills

Repealed

Section 1a. Initiative and Referendum on Parts Of Laws and on Local, Special and Municipal Laws

Repealed

Section 1b. Payment for Signatures

It shall be unlawful to pay or receive money or other thing of value based on the number of signatures obtained on an initiative or referendum petition. Nothing herein prohibits payment for signature gathering which is not based, either directly or indirectly, on the number of signatures obtained.

Section 1d. Effective Date of Amendment to Section 1, Article IV, by S.J.R. 3, 1999

Repealed

Section 2. Number of Senators and Representatives

The Senate shall consist of sixteen, and the House of Representatives of thirty four members, which number shall not be increased until the year Eighteen Hundred and Sixty, after which time the Legislative Assembly may increase the number of Senators and Representatives, always keeping as near as may be the same ratio as to the number of Senators, and Representatives: Provided that the Senate shall never exceed thirty and the House of Representatives sixty members.

Section 3. How Senators and Representatives Chosen; Filling Vacancies; Qualifications

(1) The senators and representatives shall be chosen by the electors of the respective counties or districts or sub-districts within a county or district into which the state may from time to time be divided by law.

(2)(a) If a vacancy occurs in the office of senator or representative from any county or district or sub-district, the vacancy shall be filled as may be provided by law.

(b) Except as provided in paragraph (c) of this subsection, a person who is appointed to fill a vacancy in the office of senator or representative must be an inhabitant of the district the person is appointed to represent for at least one year next preceding the date of the appointment.

(c) For purposes of an appointment occurring during the period beginning on January 1 of the year a reapportionment becomes operative under section 6 of this Article, the person must have been an inhabitant of the district for one year next preceding the date of the appointment or from January 1 of the year the reapportionment becomes operative to the date of the appointment, whichever is less.

Section 3a. Applicability of Qualifications for Appointment to Legislative Vacancy

Repealed

Section 4. Term of Office of Legislators; Classification of Senators

(1) The Senators shall be elected for the term of four years, and Representatives for the term of two years. The term of each Senator and Representative shall commence on the second Monday in January following his election, and shall continue for the full period of four years or two years, as the case may be, unless a different commencing day for such terms shall have been appointed by law.

(2) The Senators shall continue to be divided into two classes, in accordance with the division by lot provided for under the former provisions of this Constitution, so that one-half, as nearly as possible, of the number of Senators shall be elected biennially.

(3) Any Senator or Representative whose term, under the former provisions of this section, would have expired on the first Monday in January 1961, shall continue in office until the second Monday in January 1961.

Section 5. Census

Repealed

Section 6. Apportionment of Senators and Representatives

Repealed

Section 6. Apportionment of Senators and Representatives; Operative Date

(1) At the odd-numbered year regular session of the Legislative Assembly next following an enumeration of the inhabitants by the United States Government, the number of Senators and Representatives shall be fixed by law and apportioned among legislative districts according to population. A senatorial district shall consist of two representative districts. Any Senator whose term continues through the next odd-numbered year regular legislative session after the operative date of the reapportionment shall be specifically assigned to a senatorial district. The ratio of Senators and Representatives, respectively, to population shall be determined by dividing the total population of the state by the number of Senators and by the number of Representatives. A reapportionment by the Legislative Assembly becomes operative as described in subsection (6) of this section.

(2) This subsection governs judicial review and correction of a reapportionment enacted by the Legislative Assembly.

(a) Original jurisdiction is vested in the Supreme Court, upon the petition of any elector of the state filed with the Supreme Court on or before August 1 of the year in which the Legislative Assembly enacts a reapportionment, to review any reapportionment so enacted.

(b) If the Supreme Court determines that the reapportionment thus reviewed complies with subsection (1) of this section and all law applicable thereto, it shall dismiss the petition by written opinion on or before September 1 of the same year and the reapportionment becomes operative as described in subsection

(6) of this section.

(c) If the Supreme Court determines that the reapportionment does not comply with subsection (1) of this section and all law applicable thereto, the reapportionment shall be void. In its written opinion, the Supreme Court shall specify with particularity wherein the reapportionment fails to comply. The opinion shall further direct the Secretary of State to draft a reapportionment of the Senators and Representatives in accordance with the provisions of subsection (1) of this section and all law applicable thereto. The Supreme Court shall file its order with the Secretary of State on or before September 15. The Secretary of State shall conduct a hearing on the reapportionment at which the public may submit evidence, views and argument. The Secretary of State shall cause a transcription of the hearing to be prepared which, with the evidence, shall become part of the record. The Secretary of State shall file the corrected reapportionment with the Supreme Court on or before November 1 of the same year.

(d) On or before November 15, the Supreme Court shall review the corrected reapportionment to assure its compliance with subsection (1) of this section and all law applicable thereto and may further correct the reapportionment if the court considers correction to be necessary.

(e) The corrected reapportionment becomes operative as described in subsection (6) of this section.

(3) This subsection governs enactment, judicial review and correction of a reapportionment if the Legislative Assembly fails to enact any reapportionment by July 1 of the year of the odd-numbered year regular session of the Legislative Assembly next following an enumeration of the inhabitants by the United States Government.

(a) The Secretary of State shall make a reapportionment of the Senators and Representatives in accordance with the provisions of subsection (1) of this section and all law applicable thereto. The Secretary of State shall conduct a hearing on the reapportionment at which the public may submit evidence, views and argument. The Secretary of State shall cause a transcription of the hearing to be prepared which, with the evidence, shall become part of the record. The reapportionment so made shall be filed with the Supreme Court by August 15 of the same year. The reapportionment becomes operative as described in subsection (6) of this section.

(b) Original jurisdiction is vested in the Supreme Court upon the petition of any elector of the state filed with the Supreme Court on or before September 15 of the same year to review any reapportionment and the record made by the Secretary of State.

(c) If the Supreme Court determines that the reapportionment thus reviewed complies with subsection (1) of this section and all law applicable thereto, it shall dismiss the petition by written opinion on or before October 15 of the same year and the reapportionment becomes operative as described in subsection

(6) of this section.

(d) If the Supreme Court determines that the reapportionment does not comply with subsection (1) of this section and all law applicable thereto, the reapportionment shall be void. The Supreme Court shall return the reapportionment by November 1 to the Secretary of State accompanied by a written opinion specifying with particularity wherein the reapportionment fails to comply. The opinion shall further direct the Secretary of State to correct the reapportionment in those particulars, and in no others, and file the corrected reapportionment with the Supreme Court on or before December 1 of the same year.

(e) On or before December 15, the Supreme Court shall review the corrected reapportionment to assure its compliance with subsection (1) of this section and all law applicable thereto and may further correct the reapportionment if the court considers correction to be necessary.

(f) The reapportionment becomes operative as described in subsection (6) of this section.

(4) Any reapportionment that becomes operative as provided in this section is a law of the state except for purposes of initiative and referendum.

(5) Notwithstanding section 18, Article II of this Constitution, after the convening of the next odd-numbered year regular legislative session following the reapportionment, a Senator whose term continues through that legislative session is subject to recall by the electors of the district to which the Senator is assigned and not by the electors of the district existing before the latest reapportionment. The number of signatures required on the recall petition is 15 percent of the total votes cast for all candidates for Governor at the most recent election at which a candidate for Governor was elected to a full term in the two representative districts comprising the senatorial district to which the Senator was assigned.

(6)(a) Except as provided in paragraph (b) of this subsection, a reapportionment made under this section becomes operative on the second Monday in January of the next odd-numbered year after the applicable deadline for making a final reapportionment under this section.

(b) For purposes of electing Senators and Representatives to the next term of office that commences after the applicable deadline for making a final reapportionment under this section, a reapportionment made under this section becomes operative on January 1 of the calendar year next following the applicable deadline for making a final reapportionment under this section.

Section 7. Senatorial Districts; Senatorial and Representative Sub-Districts

A senatorial district, when more than one county shall constitute the same, shall be composed of contiguous counties, and no county shall be divided in creating such senatorial districts. Senatorial or representative districts comprising not more than one county may be divided into sub-districts from time to time by law. Sub-districts shall be composed of contiguous territory within the district; and the ratios to population of senators or representatives, as the case may be, elected from the sub-districts, shall be substantially equal within the district.

Section 8. Qualification of Senators and Representatives; Effect of Felony Conviction

(1)(a) Except as provided in paragraph (b) of this subsection, a person may not be a Senator or Representative if the person at the time of election:

(A) Is not a citizen of the United States; and

(B) Has not been for one year next preceding the election an inhabitant of the district from which the Senator or Representative may be chosen.

(b) For purposes of the general election next following the applicable deadline for making a final apportionment under section 6 of this Article, the person must have been an inhabitant of the district from January 1 of the year following the applicable deadline for making the final reapportionment to the date of the election.

(2) Senators and Representatives shall be at least twenty one years of age.

(3) A person may not be a Senator or Representative if the person has been convicted of a felony during:

(a) The term of office of the person as a Senator or Representative; or

(b) The period beginning on the date of the election at which the person was elected to the office of Senator or Representative and ending on the first day of the term of office to which the person was elected.

(4) A person is not eligible to be elected as a Senator or Representative if that person has been convicted of a felony and has not completed the sentence received for the conviction prior to the date that person would take office if elected. As used in this subsection, "sentence received for the conviction" includes a term of imprisonment, any period of probation or post-prison supervision and payment of a monetary obligation imposed as all or part of a sentence.

(5) Notwithstanding sections 11 and 15, Article IV of this Constitution:

(a) The office of a Senator or Representative convicted of a felony during the term to which the Senator or Representative was elected or appointed shall become vacant on the date the Senator or Representative is convicted.

(b) A person elected to the office of Senator or Representative and convicted of a felony during the period beginning on the date of the election and ending on the first day of the term of office to which the person was elected shall be ineligible to take office and the office shall become vacant on the first day of the next term of office.

(6) Subject to subsection (4) of this section, a person who is ineligible to be a Senator or Representative under subsection (3) of this section may:

(a) Be a Senator or Representative after the expiration of the term of office during which the person is ineligible; and

(b) Be a candidate for the office of Senator or Representative prior to the expiration of the term of office during which the person is ineligible.

(7)(a) Except as provided in paragraph (b) of this subsection, a person may not be a Senator or Representative if the person at all times during the term of office of the person as a Senator or Representative is not an inhabitant of the district from which the Senator or Representative may be chosen or which the Senator or Representative has been appointed to represent. A person does not lose status as an inhabitant of a district if the person is absent from the district for purposes of business of the Legislative Assembly.

(b) Following the applicable deadline for making a final apportionment under section 6 of this Article, until the expiration of the term of office of the person, a person may be an inhabitant of any district.

Section 8a. Applicability of Qualification for Legislative Office

Repealed

Section 9. Legislators Free From Arrest and Not Subject to Civil Process in Certain Cases; Words Uttered in Debate

Senators and Representatives in all cases, except for treason, felony, or breaches of the peace, shall be privileged from arrest during the session of the Legislative Assembly, and in going to and returning from the same; and shall not be subject to any civil process during the session of the Legislative Assembly, nor during the fifteen days next before the commencement thereof: Nor shall a member for words uttered in debate in either house, be questioned in any other place.

Section 10. Annual Regular Sessions of the Legislative Assembly; Organizational Session; Extension of Regular Sessions

(1) The Legislative Assembly shall hold annual sessions at the Capitol of the State. Each session must begin on the day designated by law as the first day of the session. Except as provided in subsection (3) of this section:

(a) A session beginning in an odd-numbered year may not exceed 160 calendar days in duration; and

(b) A session beginning in an even-numbered year may not exceed 35 calendar days in duration.

(2) The Legislative Assembly may hold an organizational session that is not subject to the limits of subsection (1) of this section for the purposes of introducing measures and performing the duties and effecting the organization described in sections 11 and 12 of this Article. The Legislative Assembly may not undertake final consideration of a measure or reconsideration of a measure following a gubernatorial veto when convened in an organizational session.

(3) A regular session, as described in subsection (1) of this section, may be extended for a period of five calendar days by the affirmative vote of two-thirds of the members of each house. A session may be extended more than once. An extension must begin on the first calendar day after the end of the immediately preceding session or extension except that if the first calendar day is a Sunday, the extension may begin on the next Monday.

Section 10a. Emergency Sessions of the Legislative Assembly

In the event of an emergency the Legislative Assembly shall be convened by the presiding officers of both Houses at the Capitol of the State at times other than required by section 10 of this Article upon the written request of the majority of the members of each House to commence within five days after receipt of the minimum requisite number of requests.

Section 11. Legislative Officers; Rules of Proceedings; Adjournments

Each house when assembled, shall choose its own officers, judge of the election, qualifications, and returns of its own members; determine its own rules of proceeding, and sit upon its own adjournments; but neither house shall without the concurrence of the other, adjourn for more than three days, nor to any other place than that in which it may be sitting.

Section 12. Quorum; Failure to Effect Organization

Two thirds of each house shall constitute a quorum to do business, but a smaller number may meet; adjourn from day to day, and compel the attendance of absent members. A quorum being in attendance, if either house fail to effect an organization within the first five days thereafter, the members of the house so failing shall be entitled to no compensation from the end of the said five days until an organization shall have been effected.

Section 13. Journal; When Yeas and Nays to be Entered

Each house shall keep a journal of its proceedings. The yeas and nays on any question, shall at the request of any two members, be entered, together with the names of the members demanding the same, on the journal; provided that on a motion to adjourn it shall require one tenth of the members present to order the yeas, and nays.

Section 14. Deliberations to be Open; Rules to Implement Requirement

The deliberations of each house, of committees of each house or joint committees and of committees of the whole, shall be open. Each house shall adopt rules to implement the requirement of this section and the houses jointly shall adopt rules to implement the requirements of this section in any joint activity that the two houses may undertake.

Section 15. Punishment and Expulsion of Members

Either house may punish its members for disorderly behavior, and may with the concurrence of two thirds, expel a member; but not a second time for the same cause.

Section 16. Punishment of Nonmembers

Either house, during its session, may punish by imprisonment, any person, not a member, who shall have been guilty of disrespect to the house by disorderly or contemptious [sic] behavior in its presence, but such imprisonment shall not at any time, exceed twenty [sic] twenty four hours.

Section 17. General Powers of Legislative Assembly

Each house shall have all powers necessary for a chamber of the Legislative Branch, of a free, and independent State.

Section 18. Where Bills to Originate

Bills may originate in either house, but may be amended, or rejected in the other; except that bills for raising revenue shall originate in the House of Representatives.

Section 19. Reading of Bills; Vote on Final Passage

Every bill shall be read by title only on three several days, in each house, unless in case of emergency two-thirds of the house where such bill may be pending shall, by a vote of yeas and nays, deem it expedient to dispense with this rule; provided, however, on its final passage such bill shall be read section by section unless such requirement be suspended by a vote of two-thirds of the house where such bill may be pending, and the vote on the final passage of every bill or joint resolution shall be taken by yeas and nays.

Section 20. Subject and Title of Act

Every Act shall embrace but one subject, and matters properly connected therewith, which subject shall be expressed in the title. But if any subject shall be embraced in an Act which shall not be expressed in the title, such Act shall be void only as to so much thereof as shall not be expressed in the title.
This section shall not be construed to prevent the inclusion in an amendatory Act, under a proper title, of matters otherwise germane to the same general subject, although the title or titles of the original Act or Acts may not have been sufficiently broad to have permitted such matter to have been so included in such original Act or Acts, or any of them.

Section 21. Acts to be Plainly Worded

Every act, and joint resolution shall be plainly worded, avoiding as far as practicable the use of technical terms.

Section 22. Mode of Revision and Amendment

No act shall ever be revised, or amended by mere reference to its title, but the act revised, or section amended shall be set forth, and published at full length. However, if, at any session of the Legislative Assembly, there are enacted two or more acts amending the same section, each of the acts shall be given effect to the extent that the amendments do not conflict in purpose. If the amendments conflict in purpose, the act last signed by the Governor shall control.

Section 23. Certain Local and Special Laws Prohibited

The Legislative Assembly, shall not pass special or local laws, in any of the following enumerated cases, that is to say:

Regulating the jurisdiction, and duties of justices of the peace, and of constables;

For the punishment of Crimes, and Misdemeanors;

Regulating the practice in Courts of Justice;

Providing for changing the venue in civil, and Criminal cases;

Granting divorces;

Changing the names of persons;

For laying, opening, and working on highways, and for the election, or appointment of supervisors;

Vacating roads, Town plats, Streets, Alleys, and Public squares;

Summoning and empanneling [sic] grand, and petit jurors;

For the assessment and collection of Taxes, for State, County, Township, or road purposes;

Providing for supporting Common schools, and for the preservation of school funds;

In relation to interest on money;

Providing for opening, and conducting the elections of State, County, and Township officers, and designating the places of voting;

Providing for the sale of real estate, belonging to minors, or other persons laboring under legal disabilities, by executors, administrators, guardians, or trustees.

Section 24. Suit Against State

Provision may be made by general law, for bringing suit against the State, as to all liabilities originating after, or existing at the time of the adoption of this Constitution; but no special act authorizeing [sic] such suit to be brought, or making compensation to any person claiming damages against the State, shall ever be passed.

Section 25. Majority Necessary to Pass Bills and Resolutions; Special Requirements for Bills Raising Revenue; Signatures of Presiding Officers Required

(1) Except as otherwise provided in subsection (2) of this section, a majority of all the members elected to each House shall be necessary to pass every bill or Joint resolution.

(2) Three-fifths of all members elected to each House shall be necessary to pass bills for raising revenue.

(3) All bills, and Joint resolutions passed, shall be signed by the presiding officers of the respective houses.

Section 26. Protest by Member

Any member of either house, shall have the right to protest, and have his protest, with his reasons for dissent, entered on the journal.

Section 27. All Statutes Public Laws; Exceptions

Every Statute shall be a public law, unless otherwise declared in the Statute itself.

Section 28. When Act Takes Effect

No act shall take effect, until ninety days from the end of the session at which the same shall have been passed, except in case of emergency; which emergency shall be declared in the preamble, or in the body of the law.

Section 29. Compensation of Members

The members of the Legislative Assembly shall receive for their services a salary to be established and paid in the same manner as the salaries of other elected state officers and employes.

Section 30. Members not Eligible to Other Offices

No Senator or Representative shall, during the time for which he may have been elected, be eligible to any office the election to which is vested in the Legislative Assembly; nor shall be appointed to any civil office of profit which shall have been created, or the emoluments of which shall have been increased during such term; but this latter provision shall not be construed to apply to any officer elective by the people.

Section 31. Oath of Members

The members of the Legislative Assembly shall before they enter on the duties of their respective offices, take and subscribe the following oath or affirmation;

"I do solemnly swear (or affirm as the case may be) that I will support the Constitution of the United States, and the Constitution of the State of Oregon, and that I will faithfully discharge the duties of Senator (or Representative as the case may be) according to the best of my Ability"

And such oath may be administered by the Govenor [sic], Secretary of State, or a judge of the Supreme Court.

Section 32. Income Tax Defined by Federal Law; Review of Tax Laws Required

Notwithstanding any other provision of this Constitution, the Legislative Assembly, in any law imposing a tax or taxes on, in respect to or measured by income, may define the income on, in respect to or by which such tax or taxes are imposed or measured, by reference to any provision of the laws of the United States as the same may be or become effective at any time or from time to time, and may prescribe exceptions or modifications to any such provisions. At each regular session the Legislative Assembly shall, and at any special session may, provide for a review of the Oregon laws imposing a tax upon or measured by income, but no such laws shall be amended or repealed except by a legislative Act.

Section 33. Reduction of Criminal Sentences Approved by Initiative or Referendum Process

Notwithstanding the provisions of section 25 of this Article, a two-thirds vote of all the members elected to each house shall be necessary to pass a bill that reduces a criminal sentence approved by the people under section 1 of this Article.

ARTICLE V: EXECUTIVE BRANCH

Section 1. Governor as Chief Executive; Term of Office; Period Of Eligibility

The cheif [sic] executive power of the State, shall be vested in a Governor, who shall hold his office for the term of four years; and no person shall be eligible to such office more than Eight, in any period of twelve years.

Section 2. Qualifications of Governor

No person except a citizen of the United States, shall be eligible to the Office of Governor, nor shall any person be eligible to that office who shall not have attained the age of thirty years, and who shall not have been three years next preceding his election, a resident within this State. The minimum age requirement of this section does not apply to a person who succeeds to the office of Governor under section 8a of this Article.

Section 3. Who Not Eligible

No member of Congress, or person holding any office under the United States, or under this State, or under any other power, shall fill the Office of Governor, except as may be otherwise provided in this Constitution.

Section 4. Election of Governor

The Governor shall be elected by the qualified Electors of the State at the times, and places of choosing members of the Legislative Assembly; and the returns of every Election for Governor, shall be sealed up, and transmitted to the Secretary of State; directed to the Speaker of the House of Representatives, who shall open, and publish them in the presence of both houses of the Legislative Assembly.

Section 5. Greatest Number of Votes Decisive; Election by Legislature in Case of Tie

The person having the highest number of votes for Governor, shall be elected; but in case two or more persons shall have an equal and the highest number of votes for Governor, the two houses of the Legislative Assembly at the next regular session thereof, shall forthwith by joint vote, proceed to elect one of the said persons Governor.

Section 6. Contested Elections

Contested Elections for Governor shall be determined by the Legislative Assembly in such manner as may be prescribed by law.

Section 7. Term of Office

The official term of the Governor shall be four years; and shall commence at such times as may be prescribed by this constitution, or prescribed by law.

Section 8. Vacancy in Office of Governor

Repealed

Section 8a. Vacancy in Office of Governor

In case of the removal from office of the Governor, or of his death, resignation, or disability to discharge the duties of his office as prescribed by law, the Secretary of State; or if there be none, or in case of his removal from office, death, resignation, or disability to discharge the duties of his office as prescribed by law, then the State Treasurer; or if there be none, or in case of his removal from office, death, resignation, or disability to discharge the duties of his office as prescribed by law, then the President of the Senate; or if there be none, or in case of his removal from office, death, resignation, or disability to discharge the duties of his office as prescribed by law, then the Speaker of the House of Representatives, shall become Governor until the disability be removed, or a Governor be elected at the next general biennial election. The Governor elected to fill the vacancy shall hold office for the unexpired term of the outgoing Governor. The Secretary of State or the State Treasurer shall appoint a person to fill his office until the election of a Governor, at which time the office so filled by appointment shall be filled by election; or, in the event of a disability of the Governor, to be Acting Secretary of State or Acting State Treasurer until the disability be removed. The person so appointed shall not be eligible to succeed to the office of Governor by automatic succession under this section during the term of his appointment.

Section 9. Governor as Commander in Chief of State Military Forces

The Governor shall be commander in cheif [sic] of the military, and naval forces of this State, and may call out such forces to execute the laws, to suppress insurection [sic], or to repel invasion.

Section 10. Governor to See Laws Executed

He shall take care that the Laws be faithfully executed.

Section 11. Recommendations to Legislature

He shall from time to time give to the Legislative Assembly information touching the condition of the State, and reccommend [sic] such measures as he shall judge to be expedient[.]

Section 12. Governor May Convene Legislature

He may on extraordinary occasions convene the Legislative Assembly by proclamation, and shall state to both houses when assembled, the purpose for which they shall have been convened.

Section 13. Transaction of Governmental Business

He shall transact all necessary business with the officers of government, and may require information in writing from the offices of the Administrative, and Military Departments upon any subject relating to the duties of their respective offices.

Section 14. Reprieves, Commutations and Pardons; Remission of Fines and Forfeitures

He shall have power to grant reprieves, commutations, and pardons, after conviction, for all offences [sic] except treason, subject to such regulations as may be provided by law. Upon conviction for treason he shall have power to suspend the execution of the sentence until the case shall be reported to the Legislative Assembly, at its next meeting, when the Legislative Assembly shall either grant a pardon, commute the sentence, direct the execution of the sentence, or grant a farther [sic] reprieve.

He shall have power to remit fines, and forfeitures, under such regulations as may be prescribed by law; and shall report to the Legislative Assembly at its next meeting each case of reprieve, commutation, or pardon granted, and the reasons for granting the same; and also the names of all persons in whose favor remission of fines, and forfeitures shall have been made, and the several amounts remitted[.]

Section 15. Repealed and Re-designated as Section 15b

Section 15a. Single Item and Emergency Clause Veto

The Governor shall have power to veto single items in appropriation bills, and any provision in new bills declaring an emergency, without thereby affecting any other provision of such bill.

Section 15b. Legislative Enactments; Approval by Governor; Notice of Intention to Disapprove; Disapproval and Reconsideration by Legislature; Failure of Governor to Return Bill

(1) Every bill which shall have passed the Legislative Assembly shall, before it becomes a law, be presented to the Governor; if the Governor approve, the Governor shall sign it; but if not, the Governor shall return it with written objections to that house in which it shall have originated, which house shall enter the objections at large upon the journal and proceed to reconsider it.

(2) If, after such reconsideration, two-thirds of the members present shall agree to pass the bill, it shall be sent, together with the objections, to the other house, by which it shall likewise be reconsidered, and, if approved by two-thirds of the members present, it shall become a law. But in all such cases, the votes of both houses shall be determined by yeas and nays, and the names of the members voting for or against the bill shall be entered on the journal of each house respectively.

(3) If any bill shall not be returned by the Governor within five days (Saturdays and Sundays excepted) after it shall have been presented to the Governor, it shall be a law without signature, unless the general adjournment shall prevent its return, in which case it shall be a law, unless the Governor within thirty days next after the adjournment (Saturdays and Sundays excepted) shall file such bill, with written objections thereto, in the office of the Secretary of State, who shall lay the same before the Legislative Assembly at its next session in like manner as if it had been returned by the Governor.

(4) Before filing a bill after adjournment with written objections, the Governor must announce publicly the possible intention to do so at least five days before filing the bill with written objections. However, nothing in this subsection requires the Governor to file any bill with objections because of the announcement.

Section 16. Governor to Fill Vacancies by Appointment

When during a recess of the legislative assembly a vacancy occurs in any office, the appointment to which is vested in the legislative assembly, or when at any time a vacancy occurs in any other state office, or in the office of judge of any court, the governor shall fill such vacancy by appointment, which shall expire when a successor has been elected and qualified. When any vacancy occurs in any elective office of the state or of any district or county thereof, the vacancy shall be filled at the next general election, provided such vacancy occurs more than sixty-one (61) days prior to such general election.

Section 17. Governor to Issue Writs of Election to Fill Vacancies in Legislature

He shall issue writs of Election to fill such vacancies as may have occured [sic] in the Legislative Assembly.

Section 18. Commissions

All commissions shall issue in the name of the State; shall be signed by the Govenor [sic], sealed with the seal of the State, and attested by the Secretary of State.

ARTICLE VI: ADMINISTRATIVE DEPARTMENT

Section 1. Election of Secretary and Treasurer of State; Terms of Office; Period of Eligibility

There shall be elected by the qualified electors of the State, at the times and places of choosing Members of the Legislative Assembly, a Secretary, and Treasurer of State, who shall severally hold their offices for the term of four years; but no person shall be eligible to either of said offices more than Eight in any period of Twelve years.

Section 2. Duties of Secretary of State

The Secretary of State shall keep a fair record of the official acts of the Legislative Assembly, and Executive Branch; and shall when required lay the same, and all matters relative thereto before either chamber of the Legislative Assembly. The Secretary of State shall be by virtue of holding the office, Auditor of Public Accounts, and shall perform such other duties as shall be assigned to the Secretary of State by law.

Section 3. Seal of State

There shall be a seal of State, kept by the Secretary of State for official purposes, which shall be called

"The seal of the State of Oregon".

Section 4. Powers and Duties of Treasurer.

The powers, and duties of the Treasurer of State shall be such as may be prescribed by law.

Section 5. Offices and Records of Executive Officers

The Governor, Secretary of State, and Treasurer of State shall severally keep the public records, books and papers at the seat of government in any manner relating to their respective offices.

Section 6. County Officers.

There shall be elected in each county by the qualified electors thereof at the time of holding general elections, a county clerk, treasurer and sheriff who shall severally hold their offices for the term of four years.

Section 7. Other Officers

Such other county, township, precinct, and City officers as may be necessary, shall be elected, or appointed in such manner as may be prescribed by law.

Section 8. County Officers Qualifications; Location of Offices of County and City Officers; Duties of Such Officers

Every county officer shall be an elector of the county, and the county assessor, county sheriff, county coroner and county surveyor shall possess such other qualifications as may be prescribed by law. All county and city officers shall keep their respective offices at such places therein, and perform such duties, as may be prescribed by law.

Section 9. Vacancies in County, Township, Precinct and City Offices

Vacancies in County, Township, precinct and City offices shall be filled in such manner as may be prescribed by law.

Section 9a. County Manager form of Government

Repealed

Section 10. County Home Rule Under County Charter

The Legislative Assembly shall provide by law a method whereby the legal voters of any county, by majority vote of such voters voting thereon at any legally called election, may adopt, amend, revise or repeal a county charter. A county charter may provide for the exercise by the county of authority over matters of county concern. Local improvements shall be financed only by taxes, assessments or charges imposed on benefited property, unless otherwise provided by law or charter. A county charter shall prescribe the organization of the county government and shall provide directly, or by its authority, for the number, election or appointment, qualifications, tenure, compensation, powers and duties of such officers as the county deems necessary. Such officers shall among them exercise all the powers and perform all the duties, as distributed by the county charter or by its authority, now or hereafter, by the Constitution or laws of this state, granted to or imposed upon any county officer. Except as expressly provided by general law, a county charter shall not affect the selection, tenure, compensation, powers or duties prescribed by law for judges in their judicial capacity, for justices of the peace or for district attorneys. The initiative and referendum powers reserved to the people by this Constitution hereby are further reserved to the legal voters of every county relative to the adoption, amendment, revision or repeal of a county charter and to legislation passed by counties which have adopted such a charter; and no county shall require that referendum petitions be filed less than 90 days after the provisions of the charter or the legislation proposed for referral is adopted by the county governing body. To be circulated, referendum or initiative petitions shall set forth in full the charter or legislative provisions proposed for adoption or referral. Referendum petitions shall not be required to include a ballot title to be circulated. In a county a number of signatures of qualified voters equal to but not greater than four percent of the total number of all votes cast in the county for all candidates for Governor at the election at which a Governor was elected for a term of four years next preceding the filing of the petition shall be required for a petition to order a referendum on county legislation or a part thereof. A number of signatures equal to but not greater than six percent of the total number of votes cast in the county for all candidates for Governor at the election at which a Governor was elected for a term of four years next preceding the filing of the petition shall be required for a petition to propose an initiative ordinance. A number of signatures equal to but not greater than eight percent of the total number of votes cast in the county for all candidates for Governor at the election at which a Governor was elected for a term of four years next preceding the filing of the petition shall be required for a petition to propose a charter amendment.

ARTICLE VII: JUDICIAL BRANCH

Section 1. Courts; Election of Judges; Term of Office; Compensation

The judicial power of the state shall be vested in one supreme court and in such other courts as may from time to time be created by law. The judges of the supreme and other courts shall be elected by the legal voters of the state or of their respective districts for a term of six years, and shall receive such compensation as may be provided by law, which compensation shall not be diminished during the term for which they are elected.

Section 1a. Retirement of Judges; Recall to Temporary Active Service

Notwithstanding the provisions of section 1, Article VII (Amended) of this Constitution, a judge of any court shall retire from judicial office at the end of the calendar year in which he attains the age of 75 years. The Legislative Assembly or the people may by law:

(1) Fix a lesser age for mandatory retirement not earlier than the end of the calendar year in which the judge attains the age of 70 years;

(2) Provide for recalling retired judges to temporary active service on the court from which they are retired; and

(3) Authorize or require the retirement of judges for physical or mental disability or any other cause rendering judges incapable of performing their judicial duties.
This section shall not affect the term to which any judge shall have been elected or appointed prior to or at the time of approval and ratification of this section.

Section 2. Amendment's Effect on Courts, Jurisdiction a nd Judicial System; Supreme Court's Original Jurisdiction

The courts, jurisdiction, and judicial system of Oregon, except so far as expressly changed by this amendment, shall remain as at present constituted until otherwise provided by law. But the supreme court may, in its own discretion, take original jurisdiction in mandamus, quo warranto and habeas corpus proceedings.

Section 2a. Temporary appointment and assignment of judges

The Legislative Assembly or the people may by law empower the Supreme Court to:

(1) Appoint retired judges of the Supreme Court or judges of courts inferior to the Supreme Court as temporary members of the Supreme Court.

(2) Appoint members of the bar as judges pro tempore of courts inferior to the Supreme Court.

(3) Assign judges of courts inferior to the Supreme Court to serve temporarily outside the district for which they were elected.

A judge or member of the bar so appointed or assigned shall while serving have all the judicial powers and duties of a regularly elected judge of the court to which he is assigned or appointed.

Section 2b. Inferior courts may be affected in certain respects by special or local laws

Notwithstanding the provisions of section 23, Article IV of this Constitution, laws creating courts inferior to the Supreme Court or prescribing and defining the jurisdiction of such courts or the manner in which such jurisdiction may be exercised, may be made applicable:

(1) To all judicial districts or other subdivisions of this state; or

(2) To designated classes of judicial districts or other subdivisions; or

(3) To particular judicial districts or other subdivisions.

Section 3. Jury Trial; Re-Examination of Issues by Appellate Court; Record on Appeal to Supreme Court; Affirmance Notwithstanding Error; Determination of Case by Supreme Court

In actions at law, where the value in controversy shall exceed $750, the right of trial by jury shall be preserved, and no fact tried by a jury shall be otherwise re-examined in any court of this state, unless the court can affirmatively say there is no evidence to support the verdict. Until otherwise provided by law, upon appeal of any case to the supreme court, either party may have attached to the bill of exceptions the whole testimony, the instructions of the court to the jury, and any other matter material to the decision of the appeal. If the supreme court shall be of opinion, after consideration of all the matters thus submitted, that the judgment of the court appealed from was such as should have been rendered in the case, such judgment shall be affirmed, notwithstanding any error committed during the trial; or if, in any respect, the judgment appealed from should be changed, and the supreme court shall be of opinion that it can determine what judgment should have been entered in the court below, it shall direct such judgment to be entered in the same manner and with like effect as decrees are now entered in equity cases on appeal to the supreme court. Provided, that nothing in this section shall be construed to authorize the supreme court to find the defendant in a criminal case guilty of an offense for which a greater penalty is provided than that of which the accused was convicted in the lower court.

Section 4. Supreme Court; Terms; Statements of Decisions of Court

The terms of the supreme court shall be appointed by law; but there shall be one term at the seat of government annually. At the close of each term the judges shall file with the secretary of state concise written statements of the decisions made at that term.

Section 5. Juries; Indictment; Information

Repealed

Section 5. Juries; Indictment; Information; Verdict in Civil Cases

(1) The Legislative Assembly shall provide by law for:

(a) Selecting juries and qualifications of jurors;

(b) Drawing and summoning grand jurors from the regular jury list at any time, separate from the panel of petit jurors;

(c) Impaneling more than one grand jury in a county; and

(d) The sitting of a grand jury during vacation as well as session of the court.

(2) A grand jury shall consist of seven jurors chosen by lot from the whole number of jurors in attendance at the court, five of whom must concur to find an indictment.

(3) Except as provided in subsections (4) and (5) of this section, a person shall be charged in a circuit court with the commission of any crime punishable as a felony only on indictment by a grand jury.

(4) The district attorney may charge a person on an information filed in circuit court of a crime punishable as a felony if the person appears before the judge of the circuit court and knowingly waives indictment.

(5) The district attorney may charge a person on an information filed in circuit court if, after a preliminary hearing before a magistrate, the person has been held to answer upon a showing of probable cause that a crime punishable as a felony has been committed and that the person has committed it, or if the person knowingly waives preliminary hearing.

(6) An information shall be substantially in the form provided by law for an indictment. The district attorney may file an amended indictment or information whenever, by ruling of the court, an indictment or information is held to be defective in form.

(7) In civil cases three-fourths of the jury may render a verdict.

Section 6. Incompetency or Malfeasance of Public Officer

Public officers shall not be impeached; but incompetency, corruption, malfeasance or delinquency in office may be tried in the same manner as criminal offenses, and judgment may be given of dismissal from office, and such further punishment as may have been prescribed by law.

Section 7. Oath of Office of Judges of Supreme Court

Every judge of the supreme court, before entering upon the duties of his office, shall take and subscribe, and transmit to the secretary of state, the following oath:

"I, _____, do solemnly swear (or affirm) that I will support the constitution of the United States, and the constitution of the State of Oregon, and that I will faithfully and impartially discharge the duties of a judge of the supreme court of this state, according to the best of my ability, and that I will not accept any other office, except judicial offices, during the term for which I have been elected."

Section 8. Removal, suspension or censure of judges

(1) In the manner provided by law, and notwithstanding section 1 of this Article, a judge of any court may be removed or suspended from his judicial office by the Supreme Court, or censured by the Supreme Court, for:

(a) Conviction in a court of this or any other state, or of the United States, of a crime punishable as a felony or a crime involving moral turpitude; or

(b) Willful misconduct in a judicial office where such misconduct bears a demonstrable relationship to the effective performance of judicial duties; or

(c) Willful or persistent failure to perform judicial duties; or

(d) Generally incompetent performance of judicial duties; or

(e) Willful violation of any rule of judicial conduct as shall be established by the Supreme Court; or

(f) Habitual drunkenness or illegal use of narcotic or dangerous drugs.

(2) Notwithstanding section 6 of this Article, the methods provided in this section, section 1a of this Article and in section 18, Article II of this Constitution, are the exclusive methods of the removal, suspension, or censure of a judge.

Section 9. Juries of Less Than 12 Jurors

Provision may be made by law for juries consisting of less than 12 but not less than six jurors.

ARTICLE VIII: EDUCATION AND SCHOOL LANDS

Section 1. Superintendent of Public Instruction

The Governor shall be superintendent of public instruction, and his powers, and duties in that capacity shall be such as may be prescribed by law; but after the term of five years from the adoption of this Constitution, it shall be competent for the Legislative Assembly to provide by law for the election of a superintendent, to provide for his compensation, and prescribe his powers and duties.

Section 2. Common School Fund

(1) The sources of the Common School Fund are:

(a) The proceeds of all lands granted to this state for educational purposes, except the lands granted to aid in the establishment of institutions of higher education under the Acts of February 14, 1859 (11 Stat. 383) and July 2, 1862 (12 Stat. 503).

(b) All the moneys and clear proceeds of all property which may accrue to the state by escheat.

(c) The proceeds of all gifts, devises and bequests, made by any person to the state for common school purposes.

(d) The proceeds of all property granted to the state, when the purposes of such grant shall not be stated.

(e) The proceeds of the five hundred thousand acres of land to which this state is entitled under the Act of September 4, 1841 (5 Stat. 455).

(f) The five percent of the net proceeds of the sales of public lands to which this state became entitled on her admission into the union.

(g) After providing for the cost of administration and any refunds or credits authorized by law, the proceeds from any tax or excise levied on, with respect to or measured by the extraction, production, storage, use, sale, distribution or receipt of oil or natural gas and the proceeds from any tax or excise levied on the ownership of oil or natural gas. However, the rate of such taxes shall not be greater than six percent of the market value of all oil and natural gas produced or salvaged from the earth or waters of this state as and when owned or produced. This paragraph does not include proceeds from any tax or excise as described in section 3, Article IX of this Constitution.

(2) All revenues derived from the sources mentioned in subsection (1) of this section shall become a part of the Common School Fund. The State Land Board may expend moneys in the Common School Fund to carry out its powers and duties under subsection (2) of section 5 of this Article. Unexpended moneys in the Common School Fund shall be invested as the Legislative Assembly shall provide by law and shall not be subject to the limitations of section 6, Article XI of this Constitution. The State Land Board may apply, as it considers appropriate, income derived from the investment of the Common School Fund to the operating expenses of the State Land Board in exercising its powers and duties under subsection (2) of section 5 of this Article. The remainder of the income derived from the investment of the Common School Fund shall be applied to the support of primary and secondary education as prescribed by law.

Section 3. System of Common Schools

The Legislative Assembly shall provide by law for the establishment of a uniform, and general system of Common schools.

Section 4. Distribution of School Fund Income

Provision shall be made by law for the distribution of the income of the common school fund among the several Counties of this state in proportion to the number of children resident therein between the ages, four and twenty years.

Section 5. State Land Board; Land Management

(1) The Governor, Secretary of State and State Treasurer shall constitute a State Land Board for the disposition and management of lands described in section 2 of this Article, and other lands owned by this state that are placed under their jurisdiction by law. Their powers and duties shall be prescribed by law.

(2) The board shall manage lands under its jurisdiction with the object of obtaining the greatest benefit for the people of this state, consistent with the conservation of this resource under sound techniques of land management.

Section 6. Qualifications of Electors at School Elections

Repealed

Section 7. Prohibition of Sale of State Timber Unless Timber Processed in Oregon.

(1) Notwithstanding subsection (2) of section 5 of this Article or any other provision of this Constitution, the State Land Board shall not authorize the sale or export of timber from lands described in section 2 of this Article unless such timber will be processed in Oregon. The limitation on sale or export in this subsection shall not apply to species, grades or quantities of timber which may be found by the State Land Board to be surplus to domestic needs.

(2) Notwithstanding any prior agreements or other provisions of law or this Constitution, the Legislative Assembly shall not authorize the sale or export of timber from state lands other than those described in section 2 of this Article unless such timber will be processed in Oregon. The limitation on sale or export in this subsection shall not apply to species, grades or quantities of timber which may be found by the State Forester to be surplus to domestic needs.

(3) This section first becomes operative when federal law is enacted allowing this state to exercise such authority or when a court or the Attorney General of this state determines that such authority lawfully may be exercised. [Created through S.J.R. 8, 1989, and adopted by the people June 27, 1989]

Section 8. Adequate and Equitable Funding

(1) The Legislative Assembly shall appropriate in each biennium a sum of money sufficient to ensure that the state's system of public education meets quality goals established by law, and publish a report that either demonstrates the appropriation is sufficient, or identifies the reasons for the insufficiency, its extent, and its impact on the ability of the state's system of public education to meet those goals.

(2) Consistent with such legal obligation as it may have to maintain substantial equity in state funding, the Legislative Assembly shall establish a system of Equalization Grants to eligible districts for each year in which the voters of such districts approve local option taxes as described in Article XI, section 11 (4)(a)(B) of this Constitution. The amount of such Grants and eligibility criteria shall be determined by the Legislative Assembly.

ARTICLE IX: FINANCE

Section 1. Assessment and Taxation; Uniform Rules; Uniformity of Operation of Laws

The Legislative Assembly shall, and the people through the initiative may, provide by law uniform rules of assessment and taxation. All taxes shall be levied and collected under general laws operating uniformly throughout the State.

Section 1a. Poll or Head Tax; Declaration of Emergency in Tax Laws

No poll or head tax shall be levied or collected in Oregon. The Legislative Assembly shall not declare an emergency in any act regulating taxation or exemption.

Section 1b. Ships Exempt from Taxation Until 1935

All ships and vessels of fifty tons or more capacity engaged in either passenger or freight coasting or foreign trade, whose home ports of registration are in the State of Oregon, shall be and are hereby exempted from all taxes of every kind whatsoever, excepting taxes for State purposes, until the first day of January, 1935.

Section 1c. Financing Redevelopment and Urban Renewal Projects

The Legislative Assembly may provide that the ad valorem taxes levied by any taxing unit, in which is located all or part of an area included in a redevelopment or urban renewal project, may be divided so that the taxes levied against any increase in the assessed value, as defined by law, of property in such area obtaining after the effective date of the ordinance or resolution approving the redevelopment or urban renewal plan for such area, shall be used to pay any indebtedness incurred for the redevelopment or urban renewal project. The legislature may enact such laws as may be necessary to carry out the purposes of this section.

Section 2. Legislature to Provide Revenue to Pay Current State Expenses and Interest

The Legislative Assembly shall provide for raising revenue sufficiently to defray the expenses of the State for each fiscal year, and also a sufficient sum to pay the interest on the State debt, if there be any.

Section 3. Laws Imposing Taxes; Gasoline and Motor Vehicle Taxes

Repealed

Section 3. Tax Imposed Only by Law; Statement of Purpose

No tax shall be levied except in accordance with law. Every law imposing a tax shall state distinctly the purpose to which the revenue shall be applied.

Section 3a. Use of Revenue from Taxes on Motor Vehicle Use and Fuel; Legislative Review of Allocation of Taxes Between Vehicle Classes

(1) Except as provided in subsection (2) of this section, revenue from the following shall be used exclusively for the construction, reconstruction, improvement, repair, maintenance, operation and use of public highways, roads, streets and roadside rest areas in this state:

(a) Any tax levied on, with respect to, or measured by the storage, withdrawal, use, sale, distribution, importation or receipt of motor vehicle fuel or any other product used for the propulsion of motor vehicles; and

(b) Any tax or excise levied on the ownership, operation or use of motor vehicles.

(2) Revenues described in subsection (1) of this section:

(a) May also be used for the cost of administration and any refunds or credits authorized by law.

(b) May also be used for the retirement of bonds for which such revenues have been pledged.

(c) If from levies under paragraph (b) of subsection (1) of this section on campers, motor homes, travel trailers, snowmobiles, or like vehicles, may also be used for the acquisition, development, maintenance or care of parks or recreation areas.

(d) If from levies under paragraph (b) of subsection (1) of this section on vehicles used or held out for use for commercial purposes, may also be used for enforcement of commercial vehicle weight, size, load, conformation and equipment regulation.

(3) Revenues described in subsection (1) of this section that are generated by taxes or excises imposed by the state shall be generated in a manner that ensures that the share of revenues paid for the use of light vehicles, including cars, and the share of revenues paid for the use of heavy vehicles, including trucks, is fair and proportionate to the costs incurred for the highway system because of each class of vehicle. The Legislative Assembly shall provide for a biennial review and, if necessary, adjustment, of revenue sources to ensure fairness and proportionality.

Section 3b. Rate of Levy on Oil or Natural Gas; Exception

Any tax or excise levied on, with respect to or measured by the extraction, production, storage, use, sale, distribution or receipt of oil or natural gas, or the ownership thereof, shall not be levied at a rate that is greater than six percent of the market value of all oil and natural gas produced or salvaged from the earth or waters of this state as and when owned or produced. This section does not apply to any tax or excise the proceeds of which are dedicated as described in sections 3 and 3a of this Article.

Section 4. Appropriation Necessary for Withdrawal From Treasury

No money shall be drawn from the treasury, but in pursuance of appropriations made by law.

Section 5. Publication of Accounts

An accurate statement of the receipts, and expenditures of the public money shall be published with the laws of each odd-numbered year regular session of the Legislative Assembly

Section 6. Deficiency of Funds; Tax Levy to Pay

Whenever the expenses, of any fiscal year, shall exceed the income, the Legislative Assembly shall provide for levying a tax, for the ensuing fiscal year, sufficient, with other sources of income, to pay the deficiency, as well as the estimated expense of the ensuing fiscal year.

Section 7. Appropriation Laws not to Contain Provisions on Other Subjects

Laws making appropriations, for the salaries of public officers, and other current expenses of the State, shall contain provisions upon no other subject.

Section 8. Stationery for Use of State

All stationary [sic] required for the use of the State shall be furnished by the lowest responsible bidder, under such regulations as may be prescribed by law. But no State Officer, or member of the Legislative Assembly shall be interested in any bid, or contract for furnishing such stationery.

Section 9. Taxation of Certain Benefits Prohibited

Benefits payable under the federal old age and survivors insurance program or benefits under section 3(a), 4(a) or 4(f) of the federal Railroad Retirement Act of 1974, as amended, or their successors, shall not be considered income for the purposes of any tax levied by the state or by a local government in this state. Such benefits shall not be used in computing the tax liability of any person under any such tax. Nothing in this section is intended to affect any benefits to which the beneficiary would otherwise be entitled. This section applies to tax periods beginning on or after January 1, 1986.

Section 10. Retirement Plan Contributions by Governmental Employees

(1) Notwithstanding any existing State or Federal laws, an employee of the State of Oregon or any political subdivision of the state who is a member of a retirement system or plan established by law, charter or ordinance, or who will receive a retirement benefit from a system or plan offered by the state or a political subdivision of the state, must contribute to the system or plan an amount equal to six percent of their salary or gross wage.

2. On and after January 1, 1995, the state and political subdivisions of the state shall not thereafter contract or otherwise agree to make any payment or contribution to a retirement system or plan that would have the effect of relieving an employee, regardless of when that employee was employed, of the obligation imposed by subsection (1) of this section.

3. On and after January 1, 1995, the state and political subdivisions of the state shall not thereafter contract or otherwise agree to increase any salary, benefit or other compensation payable to an employee for the purpose of offsetting or compensating an employee for the obligation imposed by subsection (1) of this section.

Section 11. Retirement Plan Rate of Return Contract Guarantee Prohibited

(1) Neither the state nor any political subdivision of the state shall contract to guarantee any rate of interest or return on the funds in a retirement system or plan established by law, charter or ordinance for the benefit of an employee of the state or a political subdivision of the state.

Section 12. Retirement not to be Increased By Unused Sick Leave

(1) Notwithstanding any existing Federal or State law, the retirement benefits of an employee of the state or any political subdivision of the state retiring on or after January 1, 1995, shall not in any way be increased as a result of or due to unused sick leave.

Section 13. Retirement Plan Restriction Severability

If any part of Sections 10, 11 or 12 of this Article is held to be unconstitutional under the Federal or State Constitution, the remaining parts shall not be affected and shall remain in full force and effect.

Section 14. Revenue Estimate; Retention of Excess Corporate Tax Revenue in General Fund for Public Education Funding; Return of Other Excess Revenue to Taxpayers; Legislative Increase in Estimate

(1) As soon as is practicable after adjournment sine die of an odd-numbered year regular session of the Legislative Assembly, the Governor shall cause an estimate to be prepared of revenues that will be received by the General Fund for the biennium beginning July 1. The estimated revenues from corporate income and excise taxes shall be separately stated from the estimated revenues from other General Fund sources.

(2) As soon as is practicable after the end of the biennium, the Governor shall cause actual collections of revenues received by the General Fund for that biennium to be determined. The revenues received from corporate income and excise taxes shall be determined separately from the revenues received from other General Fund sources.

(3) If the revenues received by the General Fund from corporate income and excise taxes during the biennium exceed the amount estimated to be received from corporate income and excise taxes for the biennium, by two percent or more, the total amount of the excess shall be retained in the General Fund and used to provide additional funding for public education, kindergarten through twelfth grade.

(4) If the revenues received from General Fund revenue sources, exclusive of those described in subsection (3) of this section, during the biennium exceed the amount estimated to be received from such sources for the biennium, by two percent or more, the total amount of the excess shall be returned to personal income taxpayers.

(5) The Legislative Assembly may enact laws:

(a) Establishing a tax credit, refund payment or other mechanism by which the excess revenues are returned to taxpayers, and establishing administrative procedures connected therewith.

(b) Allowing the excess revenues to be reduced by administrative costs associated with returning the excess revenues.

(c) Permitting a taxpayer's share of the excess revenues not to be returned to the taxpayer if the taxpayer's share is less than a de minimis amount identified by the Legislative Assembly.

(d) Permitting a taxpayer's share of excess revenues to be offset by any liability of the taxpayer for which the state is authorized to undertake collection efforts.

(6)(a) Prior to the close of a biennium for which an estimate described in subsection (1) of this section has been made, the Legislative Assembly, by a two-thirds majority vote of all members elected to each House, may enact legislation declaring an emergency and increasing the amount of the estimate prepared pursuant to subsection (1) of this section.

(b) The prohibition against declaring an emergency in an act regulating taxation or exemption in section 1a, Article IX of this Constitution, does not apply to legislation enacted pursuant to this subsection.

(7) This section does not apply:

(a) If, for a biennium or any portion of a biennium, a state tax is not imposed on or measured by the income of individuals.

(b) To revenues derived from any minimum tax imposed on corporations for the privilege of carrying on or doing business in this state that is imposed as a fixed amount and that is non-apportioned (except for changes of accounting periods).

(c) To biennia beginning before July 1, 2001.

Section 15. Prohibition on Tax, Fee or Other Assessment Upon Transfer of Interest in Real Property; Exception

The state, a city, county, district or other political subdivision or municipal corporation of this state shall not impose, by ordinance or other law, a tax, fee or other assessment upon the transfer of any interest in real property, or measured by the consideration paid or received upon the transfer of any interest in real property. This section does not apply to any tax, fee or other assessment in effect and operative on December 31, 2009.

ARTICLE X: THE MILITIA

Section 1. State Militia

The Legislative Assembly shall provide by law for the organization, maintenance and discipline of a state militia for the defense and protection of the State.

Section 2. Persons Exempt

Persons whose religious tenets, or conscientious scruples forbid them to bear arms shall not be compelled to do so.

Section 3. Officers

The Governor, in his capacity as Commander-in-Chief of the military forces of the State, shall appoint and commission an Adjutant General. All other officers of the militia of the State shall be appointed and commissioned by the Governor upon the recommendation of the Adjutant General.

Section 4. Staff Officers; Commissions

Repealed

Section 5. Legislature to Make Regulations for Militia

Repealed

Section 6. Continuity of Government in Event of Enemy Attack

Repealed

ARTICLE X-A: CATASTROPHIC DISASTERS

Section 1. Definitions; Declaration of Catastrophic Disaster; Convening of Legislative Assembly

(1) As used in this Article, "catastrophic disaster" means a natural or human-caused event that:

(a) Results in extraordinary levels of death, injury, property damage or disruption of daily life in this state; and

(b) Severely affects the population, infrastructure, environment, economy or government functioning of this state.

(2) As used in this Article, "catastrophic disaster" includes, but is not limited to, any of the following events if the event meets the criteria listed in subsection (1) of this section:

(a) Act of terrorism.

(b) Earthquake.

(c) Flood.

(d) Public health emergency.

(e) Tsunami.

(f) Volcanic eruption.

(g) War.

(3) The Governor may invoke the provisions of this Article if the Governor finds and declares that a catastrophic disaster has occurred. A finding required by this subsection shall specify the nature of the catastrophic disaster.

(4) At the time the Governor invokes the provisions of this Article under subsection (3) of this section, the Governor shall issue a proclamation convening the Legislative Assembly under section 12, Article V of this Constitution, unless:

(a) The Legislative Assembly is in session at the time the catastrophic disaster is declared; or

(b) The Legislative Assembly is scheduled to convene in regular session within 30 days after the date the catastrophic disaster is declared.

(5) If the Governor declares that a catastrophic disaster has occurred, the Governor shall manage the immediate response to the disaster. The actions of the Legislative Assembly under sections 3 and 4 of this Article are limited to actions necessary to implement the Governor's immediate response to the disaster and to actions necessary to aid recovery from the disaster.

Section 2. Additional Powers of Governor; Use of General Fund Moneys and Lottery Funds

(1) If the Governor declares that a catastrophic disaster has occurred, the Governor may:

(a) Use moneys appropriated from the General Fund to executive agencies for the current biennium to respond to the catastrophic disaster, regardless of the legislatively expressed purpose of the appropriation at the time the appropriation was made.

(b) Use lottery funds allocated to executive agencies for the current biennium to respond to the catastrophic disaster, regardless of the legislatively expressed purpose of the allocation at the time the allocation was made. The Governor may not reallocate lottery funds under this paragraph for purposes not authorized by section 4, Article XV of this Constitution.

(2) The authority granted to the Governor by this section terminates upon the taking effect of a law enacted after the declaration of a catastrophic disaster that specifies purposes for which appropriated General Fund moneys or allocated lottery funds may be used, or upon the date on which the provisions of sections 1 to 5 of this Article cease to be operative as provided in section 6 of this Article, whichever is sooner.

Section 3. Procedural Requirements for Legislative Assembly

If the Governor declares that a catastrophic disaster has occurred:

(1) Notwithstanding sections 10 and 10a, Article IV of this Constitution, the Legislative Assembly may convene in a place other than the Capitol of the State if the Governor or the Legislative Assembly determines that the Capitol is inaccessible.

(2) Notwithstanding section 12, Article IV of this Constitution, during any period of time when members of the Legislative Assembly are unable to compel the attendance of two-thirds of the members of each house because the catastrophic disaster has made it impossible to locate members or impossible for them to attend, two-thirds of the members of each house who are able to attend shall constitute a quorum to do business.

(3) In a session of the Legislative Assembly that is called because of the catastrophic disaster or that was imminent or ongoing at the time the catastrophic disaster was declared, the number of members of each house that constitutes a quorum under subsection (2) of this section may suspend the rule regarding reading of bills under the same circumstances and in the same manner that two-thirds of the members may suspend the rule under section 19, Article IV of this Constitution.

(4) Notwithstanding section 25, Article IV of this Constitution, during any period of time when members of the Legislative Assembly are unable to compel the attendance of two-thirds of the members of each house because the catastrophic disaster has made it impossible to locate members or impossible for them to attend, three-fifths of the members of each house who are able to attend a session described in subsection (3) of this section shall be necessary to pass every bill or joint resolution.

(5) Notwithstanding section 1a, Article IX of this Constitution, the Legislative Assembly may declare an emergency in any bill regulating taxation or exemption, including but not limited to any bill that decreases or suspends taxes or postpones the due date of taxes, if the Legislative Assembly determines that the enactment of the bill is necessary to provide an adequate response to the catastrophic disaster.

Section 4. Additional Powers of Legislative Assembly

(1) If the Governor declares that a catastrophic disaster has occurred:

(a) The Legislative Assembly may enact laws authorizing the use of revenue described in section 3a, Article IX of this Constitution, for purposes other than those described in that section.

(b) The Legislative Assembly may, by a vote of the number of members of each house that constitutes a quorum under subsection (2) of section 3 of this Article, appropriate moneys that would otherwise be returned to taxpayers under section 14, Article IX of this Constitution, to state agencies for the purpose of responding to the catastrophic disaster.

(c) Notwithstanding section 7, Article XI of this Constitution, the Legislative Assembly may lend the credit of the state or create debts or liabilities in an amount the Legislative Assembly considers necessary to provide an adequate response to the catastrophic disaster.

(d) The provisions of section 15, Article XI of this Constitution, do not apply to any law that is approved by three-fifths of the members of each house who are able to attend a session described in subsection (3) of section 3 of this Article.

(e) The Legislative Assembly may take action described in subsection (6) of section 15, Article XI of this Constitution, upon approval by three-fifths of the members of each house who are able to attend a session described in subsection (3) of section 3 of this Article.

(f) Notwithstanding section 4, Article XV of this Constitution, the Legislative Assembly may allocate proceeds from the State Lottery for any purpose and in any ratio the Legislative Assembly determines necessary to provide an adequate response to the catastrophic disaster.

(2) Nothing in this section overrides or otherwise affects the provisions of section 15b, Article V of this Constitution.

Section 5. Participation in Session of Legislative Assembly by Electronic or Other Means

For purposes of sections 3 and 4 of this Article, a member of the Legislative Assembly who cannot be physically present at a session convened under section 1 of this Article shall be considered in attendance if the member is able to participate in the session through electronic or other means that enable the member to hear or read the proceedings as the proceedings are occurring and enable others to hear or read the member's votes or other contributions as the votes or other contributions are occurring.

Section 6. Termination of Operation of This Article; Extension by Legislative Assembly; Transition Provisions; Limitation on Power of Governor to Invoke This Article

(1) Except as provided in subsection (2) of this section, the provisions of sections 1 to 5 of this Article, once invoked, shall cease to be operative not later than 30 days following the date the Governor invoked the provisions of sections 1 to 5 of this Article, or on an earlier date recommended by the Governor and determined by the Legislative Assembly. The Governor may not recommend a date under this subsection unless the Governor finds and declares that the immediate response to the catastrophic disaster has ended.

(2) Prior to expiration of the 30-day limit established in subsection (1) of this section, the Legislative Assembly may extend the operation of sections 1 to 5 of this Article beyond the 30-day limit upon the approval of three-fifths of the members of each house who are able to attend a session described in subsection (3) of section 3 of this Article.

(3) The determination by the Legislative Assembly required by subsection (1) of this section or an extension described in subsection (2) of this section shall take the form of a bill. A bill that extends the operation of sections 1 to 5 of this Article shall establish a date upon which the provisions of sections 1 to 5 of this Article shall cease to be operative. A bill described in this subsection shall be presented to the Governor for action in accordance with section 15b, Article V of this Constitution.

(4) A bill described in subsection (3) of this section may include any provisions the Legislative Assembly considers necessary to provide an orderly transition to compliance with the requirements of this Constitution that have been overridden under this Article because of the Governor's declaration of a catastrophic disaster.

(5) The Governor may not invoke the provisions of sections 1 to 5 of this Article more than one time with respect to the same catastrophic disaster. A determination under subsection (1) of this section or an extension described in subsection (2) of this section that establishes a date upon which the provisions of sections 1 to 5 of this Article shall cease to be operative does not prevent invoking the provisions of sections 1 to 5 of this Article in response to a new declaration by the Governor that a different catastrophic disaster has occurred.

ARTICLE XI: CORPORATIONS AND INTERNAL IMPROVEMENTS

Section 1. Prohibition of State Banks

The Legislative Assembly shall not have the power to establish, or incorporate any bank or banking company, or monied [sic] institution whatever; nor shall any bank company, or instition [sic] exist in the State, with the privilege of making, issuing, or putting in circulation, any bill, check, certificate, prommisory [sic] note, or other paper, or the paper of any bank company, or person, to circulate as money.

Section 2. Formation of Corporations; Municipal Charters; Intoxicating Liquor Regulation

Corporations may be formed under general laws, but shall not be created by the Legislative Assembly by special laws. The Legislative Assembly shall not enact, amend or repeal any charter or act of incorporation for any municipality, city or town. The legal voters of every city and town are hereby granted power to enact and amend their municipal charter, subject to the Constitution and criminal laws of the State of Oregon, and the exclusive power to license, regulate, control, or to suppress or prohibit, the sale of intoxicating liquors therein is vested in such municipality; but such municipality shall within its limits be subject to the provisions of the local option law of the State of Oregon.

Section 2a. Merger of Adjoining Municipalities; County-City Consolidation

(1) The Legislative Assembly, or the people by the Initiative, may enact a general law providing a method whereby an incorporated city or town or municipal corporation may surrender its charter and be merged into an adjoining city or town, provided a majority of the electors of each of the incorporated cities or towns or municipal corporations affected authorize the surrender or merger, as the case may be.

(2) In all counties having a city therein containing over 300,000 inhabitants, the county and city government thereof may be consolidated in such manner as may be provided by law with one set of officers. The consolidated county and city may be incorporated under general laws providing for incorporation for municipal purposes. The provisions of this Constitution applicable to cities, and also those applicable to counties, so far as not inconsistent or prohibited to cities, shall be applicable to such consolidated government.

Section 3. Liability of Stockholders

The stockholders of all corporations and joint stock companies shall be liable for the indebtedness of said corporation to the amount of their stock subscribed and unpaid and no more, excepting that the stockholders of corporations or joint stock companies conducting the business of banking shall be individually liable equally and ratably and not one for another, for the benefit of the depositors of said bank, to the amount of their stock, at the par value thereof, in addition to the par value of such shares, unless such banking corporation shall have provided security through membership in the federal deposit insurance corporation or other instrumentality of the United States or otherwise for the benefit of the depositors of said bank equivalent in amount to such double liability of said stockholders.

Section 4. Compensation for Property Taken by Corporation

No person's property shall be taken by any corporation under authority of law, without compensation being first made, or secured in such manner as may be prescribed by law.

Section 5. Restriction of Municipal Powers in Acts of Incorporation

Acts of the Legislative Assembly, incorporating towns, and cities, shall restrict their powers of taxation, borrowing money, contracting debts, and loaning their credit.

Section 6. State Not To Be Stockholder In Company; Exceptions; Inapplicability To Public Universities

(1) Except as provided in subsection (3) of this section, the. state shall not subscribe to, or be interested in the stock of any company, association or corporation. However, as provided by law the state may hold and dispose of stock, including stock already received, that is donated or bequeathed; and may invest, in the stock of any company, association or corporation, any funds or moneys that:

(a) Are donated or bequeathed for higher education purposes;

(b) Are the proceeds from the disposition of stock that is donated or bequeathed for higher education purposes, including stock already received; or

(c) Are dividends paid with respect to stock that is donated or bequeathed for higher education purposes, including stock already received.

(2) Notwithstanding the limits contained in subsection (1) of this section, the state may hold and dispose of stock:

(a) Received in exchange for technology created in whole or in part by a public institution of post-secondary education; or

(b) Received prior to December 5, 2002, as a state asset invested in the creation or development of technology or resources within Oregon.

(3) Subsections (1) and (2) of this section do not apply to public universities.

Section 7. Credit of State Not to Be Loaned; Limitation Upon Power of Contracting Debts

The Legislative Assembly shall not lend the credit of the state nor in any manner create any debt or liabilities which shall singly or in the aggregate with previous debts or liabilities exceed the sum of fifty thousand dollars, except in case of war or to repel invasion or suppress insurrection or to build and maintain permanent roads; and the Legislative Assembly shall not lend the credit of the state nor in any manner create any debts or liabilities to build and maintain permanent roads which shall singly or in the aggregate with previous debts or liabilities incurred for that purpose exceed one percent of the true cash value of all the property of the state taxed on an ad valorem basis; and every contract of indebtedness entered into or assumed by or on behalf of the state in violation of the provisions of this section shall be void and of no effect. This section does not apply to any agreement entered into pursuant to law by the state or any agency thereof for the lease of real property to the state or agency for any period not exceeding 20 years and for a public purpose.

Section 8. State not to Assume Debts of Counties, Towns or Other Corporations

The State shall never assume the debts of any county, town, or other corporation whatever, unless such debts, shall have been created to repel invasion, suppress insurrection, or defend the State in war.

Section 9. Limitations on Powers of County or City to Assist Corporations

No county, city, town or other municipal corporation, by vote of its citizens, or otherwise, shall become a stockholder in any joint company, corporation or association, whatever, or raise money for, or loan its credit to, or in aid of, any such company, corporation or association. Provided, that any municipal corporation designated as a port under any general or special law of the state of Oregon, may be empowered by statute to raise money and expend the same in the form of a bonus to aid in establishing water transportation lines between such port and any other domestic or foreign port or ports, and to aid in establishing water transportation lines on the interior rivers of this state, or on the rivers between Washington and Oregon, or on the rivers of Washington and Idaho reached by navigation from Oregon's rivers; any debts of a municipality to raise money created for the aforesaid purpose shall be incurred only on approval of a majority of those voting on the question, and shall not, either singly or in the aggregate, with previous debts and liabilities incurred for that purpose, exceed one per cent of the assessed valuation of all property in the municipality.

Section 10. County Debt Limitation

No county shall create any debt or liabilities which shall singly or in the aggregate, with previous debts or liabilities, exceed the sum of $5,000; provided, however, counties may incur bonded indebtedness in excess of such $5,000 limitation to carry out purposes authorized by statute, such bonded indebtedness not to exceed limits fixed by statute.

Section 11. Tax and Indebtedness Limitation

Repealed

Section 11. Tax Base Limitation

Repealed

Section 11. Property Tax Limitations on Assessed Value and Rate of Tax; Exceptions

(1)(a) For the tax year beginning July 1, 1997, each unit of property in this state shall have a maximum assessed value for ad valorem property tax purposes that does not exceed the property's real market value for the tax year beginning July 1, 1995, reduced by 10 percent.

(b) For tax years beginning after July 1, 1997, the property's maximum assessed value shall not increase by more than three percent from the previous tax year.

(c) Notwithstanding paragraph (a) or (b) of this subsection, property shall be valued at the ratio of average maximum assessed value to average real market value of property located in the area in which the property is located that is within the same property class, if on or after July 1, 1995:

(A) The property is new property or new improvements to property;

(B) The property is partitioned or subdivided;

(C) The property is rezoned and used consistently with the rezoning;

(D) The property is first taken into account as omitted property;

(E) The property becomes disqualified from exemption, partial exemption or special assessment; or

(F) A lot line adjustment is made with respect to the property, except that the total assessed value of all property affected by a lot line adjustment shall not exceed the total maximum assessed value of the affected property under paragraph (a) or (b) of this subsection.

(d) Property shall be valued under paragraph (c) of this subsection only for the first tax year in which the changes described in paragraph (c) of this subsection are taken into account following the effective date of this section. For each tax year thereafter, the limits described in paragraph (b) of this subsection apply.
(e) The Legislative Assembly shall enact laws that establish property classes and areas sufficient to make a determination under paragraph (c) of this subsection.

(f) Each property's assessed value shall not exceed the property's real market value.

(g) There shall not be a reappraisal of the real market value used in the tax year beginning July 1, 1995, for purposes of determining the property's maximum assessed value under paragraph (a) of this subsection.

(2) The maximum assessed value of property that is assessed under a partial exemption or special assessment law shall be determined by applying the percentage reduction of paragraph (a) and the limit of paragraph (b) of subsection (1) of this section, or if newly eligible for partial exemption or special assessment, using a ratio developed in a manner consistent with paragraph (c) of subsection (1) of this section to the property's partially exempt or specially assessed value in the manner provided by law. After disqualification from partial exemption or special assessment, any additional taxes authorized by law may be imposed, but in the aggregate may not exceed the amount that would have been imposed under this section had the property not been partially exempt or specially assessed for the years for which the additional taxes are being collected.

(3)(a)(A) The Legislative Assembly shall enact laws to reduce the amount of ad valorem property taxes imposed by local taxing districts in this state so that the total of all ad valorem property taxes imposed in this state for the tax year beginning July 1, 1997, is reduced by 17 percent from the total of all ad valorem property taxes that would have been imposed under repealed sections 11 and 11a of this Article (1995 Edition) and section 11b of this Article but not taking into account Ballot Measure 47 (1996), for the tax year beginning July 1, 1997.

(B) The ad valorem property taxes to be reduced under subparagraph (A) of this paragraph are those taxes that would have been imposed under repealed sections 11 or 11a of this Article (1995 Edition) or section 11b of this Article, as modified by subsection (11) of this section, other than taxes described in subsection (4), (5), (6) or (7) of this section, taxes imposed to pay bonded indebtedness described in section 11b of this Article, as modified by paragraph (d) of subsection (11) of this section, or taxes described in section 1c, Article IX of this Constitution.

(C) It shall be the policy of this state to distribute the reductions caused by this paragraph so as to reflect:

(i) The lesser of ad valorem property taxes imposed for the tax year beginning July 1, 1995, reduced by 10 percent, or ad valorem property taxes imposed for the tax year beginning July 1, 1994;

(ii) Growth in new value under subparagraph (A), (B), (C), (D) or
(E) of paragraph (c) of subsection (1) of this section, as added to the assessment and tax rolls for the tax year beginning July 1, 1996, or July 1, 1997 (or, if applicable, for the tax year beginning July 1, 1995); and

(iii) Ad valorem property taxes authorized by voters to be imposed in tax years beginning on or after July 1, 1996, and imposed according to that authority for the tax year beginning July 1, 1997.

(D) It shall be the policy of this state and the local taxing districts of this state to prioritize public safety and public education in responding to the reductions caused by this paragraph while minimizing the loss of decision-making control of local taxing districts.

(E) If the total value for the tax year beginning July 1, 1997, of additions of value described in subparagraph (A), (B), (C), (D) or (E) of paragraph (c) of subsection (1) of this section that are added to the assessment and tax rolls for the tax year beginning July 1, 1996, or July 1, 1997, exceeds four percent of the total assessed value of property statewide for the tax year beginning July 1, 1997 (before taking into account the additions of value described in subparagraph (A), (B), (C), (D) or (E) of paragraph (c) of subsection (1) of this section), then any ad valorem property taxes attributable to the excess above four percent shall reduce the dollar amount of the reduction described in subparagraph (A) of this paragraph.

(b) For the tax year beginning July 1, 1997, the ad valorem property taxes that were reduced under paragraph (a) of this subsection shall be imposed on the assessed value of property in a local taxing district as provided by law, and the rate of the ad valorem property taxes imposed under this paragraph shall be the local taxing district's permanent limit on the rate of ad valorem property taxes imposed by the district for tax years beginning after July 1, 1997, except as provided in subsection (5) of this section.

(c)(A) A local taxing district that has not previously imposed ad valorem property taxes and that seeks to impose ad valorem property taxes shall establish a limit on the rate of ad valorem property tax to be imposed by the district. The rate limit established under this subparagraph shall be approved by a majority of voters voting on the question. The rate limit approved under this subparagraph shall serve as the district's permanent rate limit under paragraph (b) of this subsection.

(B) The voter participation requirements described in subsection (8) of this section apply to an election under this paragraph.

(d) If two or more local taxing districts seek to consolidate or merge, the limit on the rate of ad valorem property tax to be imposed by the consolidated or merged district shall be the rate that would produce the same tax revenue as the local taxing districts would have cumulatively produced in the year of consolidation or merger, if the consolidation or merger had not occurred.

(e)(A) If a local taxing district divides, the limit on the rate of ad valorem property tax to be imposed by each local taxing district after division shall be the same as the local taxing district's rate limit under paragraph (b) of this subsection prior to division.

(B) Notwithstanding subparagraph (A) of this paragraph, the limit determined under this paragraph shall not be greater than the rate that would have produced the same amount of ad valorem property tax revenue in the year of division, had the division not occurred.

(f) Rates of ad valorem property tax established under this subsection may be carried to a number of decimal places provided by law and rounded as provided by law.

(g) Urban renewal levies described in this subsection shall be imposed as provided in subsections (15) and (16) of this section and may not be imposed under this subsection.

(h) Ad valorem property taxes described in this subsection shall be subject to the limitations described in section 11b of this Article, as modified by subsection (11) of this section.

(4)(a)(A) A local taxing district other than a school district may impose a local option ad valorem property tax that exceeds the limitations imposed under this section by submitting the question of the levy to voters in the local taxing district and obtaining the approval of a majority of the voters voting on the question.

(B) The Legislative Assembly may enact laws permitting a school district to impose a local option ad valorem property tax as otherwise provided under this subsection.

(b) A levy imposed pursuant to legislation enacted under this subsection may be imposed for no more than five years, except that a levy for a capital project may be imposed for no more than the lesser of the expected useful life of the capital project or 10 years.

(c) The voter participation requirements described in subsection (8) of this section apply to an election held under this subsection.

(5)(a) Any portion of a local taxing district levy shall not be subject to reduction and limitation under paragraphs (a) and (b) of subsection (3) of this section If that portion of the levy is used to repay:

(A) Principal and interest for any bond issued before December 5, 1996, and secured by a pledge or explicit commitment of ad valorem property taxes or a covenant to levy or collect ad valorem property taxes;

(B) Principal and interest for any other formal, written borrowing of moneys executed before December 5, 1996, for which ad valorem property tax revenues have been pledged or explicitly committed, or that are secured by a covenant to levy or collect ad valorem property taxes;

(C) Principal and interest for any bond issued to refund an obligation described in subparagraph (A) or (B) of this paragraph; or

(D) Local government pension and disability plan obligations that commit ad valorem property taxes and to ad valorem property taxes imposed to fulfill those obligations.

(b)(A) A levy described in this subsection shall be imposed on assessed value as otherwise provided by law in an amount sufficient to repay the debt described in this subsection. Ad valorem property taxes may not be imposed under this subsection that repay the debt at an earlier date or on a different schedule than established in the agreement creating the debt.

(B) A levy described in this subsection shall be subject to the limitations imposed under section 11b of this Article, as modified by subsection (11) of this section.

(c)(A) As used in this subsection, "local government pension and disability plan obligations that commit ad valorem property taxes" is limited to contractual obligations for which the levy of ad valorem property taxes has been committed by a local government charter provision that was in effect on December 5, 1996, and, if in effect on December 5, 1996, as amended thereafter.

(B) The rates of ad valorem property taxes described in this paragraph may be adjusted so that the maximum allowable rate is capable of raising the revenue that the levy would have been authorized to raise if applied to property valued at real market value.

(C) Notwithstanding subparagraph (B) of this paragraph, ad valorem property taxes described in this paragraph shall be taken into account for purposes of the limitations in section 11b of this Article, as modified by subsection (11) of this section.

(D) If any proposed amendment to a charter described in subparagraph (A) of this paragraph permits the ad valorem property tax levy for local government pension and disability plan obligations to be increased, the amendment must be approved by voters in an election. The voter participation requirements described in subsection (8) of this section apply to an election under this subparagraph. No amendment to any charter described in this paragraph may cause ad valorem property taxes to exceed the limitations of section 11b of this Article, as amended by subsection (11) of this section.

(d) If the levy described in this subsection was a tax base or other permanent continuing levy, other than a levy imposed for the purpose described in subparagraph (D) of paragraph (a) of this subsection, prior to the effective date of this section, for the tax year following the repayment of debt described in this subsection the local taxing district's rate of ad valorem property tax established under paragraph (b) of subsection (3) of this section shall be increased to the rate that would have been in effect had the levy not been excepted from the reduction described in subsection (3) of this section. No adjustment shall be made to the rate of ad valorem property tax of local taxing districts other than the district imposing a levy under this subsection.

(e) If this subsection would apply to a levy described in paragraph (d) of this subsection, the local taxing district imposing the levy may elect out of the provisions of this subsection. The levy of a local taxing district making the election shall be included in the reduction and ad valorem property tax rate determination described in subsection (3) of this section.

(6)(a) The ad valorem property tax of a local taxing district, other than a city, county or school district, that is used to support a hospital facility shall not be subject to the reduction described in paragraph (a) of subsection (3) of this section. The entire ad valorem property tax imposed under this subsection for the tax year beginning July 1, 1997, shall be the local taxing district's permanent limit on the rate of ad valorem property taxes imposed by the district under paragraph (b) of subsection (3) of this section.

(b) Ad valorem property taxes described in this subsection shall be subject to the limitations imposed under section 11b of this Article, as modified by subsection (11) of this section.

(7) Notwithstanding any other existing or former provision of this Constitution, the following are validated, ratified, approved and confirmed:
(a) Any levy of ad valorem property taxes approved by a majority of voters voting on the question in an election held before December 5, 1996, if the election met the voter participation requirements described in subsection (8) of this section and the ad valorem property taxes were first imposed for the tax year beginning July 1, 1996, or July 1, 1997. A levy described in this paragraph shall not be subject to reduction under paragraph (a) of subsection (3) of this section but shall be taken into account in determining the local taxing district's permanent rate of ad valorem property tax under paragraph (b) of subsection (3) this section. This paragraph does not apply to levies described in subsection (5) of this section or to levies to pay bonded indebtedness described in section 11b of this Article, as modified by subsection (11) of this section.

(b) Any serial or one-year levy to replace an existing serial or one-year levy approved by a majority of the voters voting on the question at an election held after December 4, 1996, and to be first imposed for the tax year beginning July 1, 1997, if the rate or the amount of the levy approved is not greater than the rate or the amount of the levy replaced.

(c) Any levy of ad valorem property taxes approved by a majority of voters voting on the question in an election held on or after December 5, 1996, and before the effective date of this section if the election met the voter participation requirements described in subsection (8) of this section and the ad valorem property taxes were first imposed for the tax year beginning July 1, 1997. A levy described in this paragraph shall be treated as a local option ad valorem property tax under subsection (4) of this section. This paragraph does not apply to levies described in subsection (5) of this section or to levies to pay bonded indebtedness described in section 11b of this Article, as modified by subsection (11) of this section.

(8) An election described in subsection (3), (4), (5)(c)(D), (7)(a) or (c) or (11) of this section shall authorize the matter upon which the election is being held only if:
(a) At least 50 percent of registered voters eligible to vote in the election cast a ballot; or

(b) The election is a general election in an even-numbered year.

(9) The Legislative Assembly shall replace, from the state's General Fund, revenue lost by the public school system because of the limitations of this section. The amount of the replacement revenue shall not be less than the total replaced in fiscal year 1997-1998.

(10)(a) As used in this section:

(A) "Improvements" includes new construction, reconstruction, major additions, remodeling, renovation and rehabilitation, including installation, but does not include minor construction or ongoing maintenance and repair.

(B) "Ad valorem property tax" does not include taxes imposed to pay principal and interest on bonded indebtedness described in paragraph (d) of subsection (11) of this section.

(b) In calculating the addition to value for new property and improvements, the amount added shall be net of the value of retired property.

(11) For purposes of this section and for purposes of implementing the limits in section 11b of this Article in tax years beginning on or after July 1, 1997:

(a)(A) The real market value of property shall be the amount in cash that could reasonably be expected to be paid by an informed buyer to an informed seller, each acting without compulsion in an arm's length transaction occurring as of the assessment date for the tax year, as established by law.

(B) The Legislative Assembly shall enact laws to adjust the real market value of property to reflect a substantial casualty loss of value after the assessment date.

(b) The $5 (public school system) and $10 (other government) limits on property taxes per $1,000 of real market value described in subsection (1) of section 11b of this Article shall be determined on the basis of property taxes imposed in each geographic area taxed by the same local taxing districts.

(c)(A) All property taxes described in this section are subject to the limits described in paragraph (b) of this subsection, except for taxes described in paragraph (d) of this subsection.

(B) If property taxes exceed the limitations imposed under either category of local taxing district under paragraph (b) of this subsection:

(i) Any local option ad valorem property taxes imposed under this subsection shall be proportionally reduced by those local taxing districts within the category that is imposing local option ad valorem property taxes; and

(ii) After local option ad valorem property taxes have been eliminated, all other ad valorem property taxes shall be proportionally reduced by those taxing districts within the category, until the limits are no longer exceeded.

(C) The percentages used to make the proportional reductions under subparagraph (B) of this paragraph shall be calculated separately for each category.

(d) Bonded indebtedness, the taxes of which are not subject to limitation under this section or section 11b of this Article, consists of:

(A) Bonded indebtedness authorized by a provision of this Constitution;

(B) Bonded indebtedness issued on or before November 6, 1990; or

(C) Bonded indebtedness:

(i) Incurred for capital construction or capital improvements; and

(ii)(I) If issued after November 6, 1990, and approved prior to December 5, 1996, the issuance of which has been approved by a majority of voters voting on the question; or

(II) If approved by voters after December 5, 1996, the issuance of which has been approved by a majority of voters voting on the question in an election that is in compliance with the voter participation requirements in subsection (8) of this section.

(12) Bonded indebtedness described in subsection (11) of this section includes bonded indebtedness issued to refund bonded indebtedness described in subsection (11) of this section.

(13) As used in subsection (11) of this section, with respect to bonded indebtedness issued on or after December 5, 1996, "capital construction" and "capital improvements":

(a) Include public safety and law enforcement vehicles with a projected useful life of five years or more; and

(b) Do not include:

(A) Maintenance and repairs, the need for which could reasonably be anticipated.

(B) Supplies and equipment that are not intrinsic to the structure.

(14) Ad valorem property taxes imposed to pay principal and interest on bonded indebtedness described in section 11b of this Article, as modified by subsection (11) of this section, shall be imposed on the assessed value of the property determined under this section or, in the case of specially assessed property, as otherwise provided by law or as limited by this section, whichever is applicable.

(15) If ad valorem property taxes are divided as provided in section 1c, Article IX of this Constitution, in order to fund a redevelopment or urban renewal project, then notwithstanding subsection (1) of this section, the ad valorem property taxes levied against the increase shall be used exclusively to pay any indebtedness incurred for the redevelopment or urban renewal project.

(16) The Legislative Assembly shall enact laws that allow collection of ad valorem property taxes sufficient to pay, when due, indebtedness incurred to carry out urban renewal plans existing on December 5, 1996. These collections shall cease when the indebtedness is paid. Unless excepted from limitation under section 11b of this Article, as modified by subsection (11) of this section, nothing in this subsection shall be construed to remove ad valorem property taxes levied against the increase from the dollar limits in paragraph (b) of subsection (11) of this section.

(17)(a) If, in an election on November 5, 1996, voters approved a new tax base for a local taxing district under repealed section 11 of this Article (1995 Edition) that was not to go into effect until the tax year beginning July 1, 1998, the local taxing district's permanent rate limit under subsection (3) of this section shall be recalculated for the tax year beginning on July 1, 1998, to reflect:

(A) Ad valorem property taxes that would have been imposed had repealed section 11 of this Article (1995 Edition) remained in effect; and

(B) Any other permanent continuing levies that would have been imposed under repealed section 11 of this Article (1995 Edition), as reduced by subsection (3) of this section.

(b) The rate limit determined under this subsection shall be the local taxing district's permanent rate limit for tax years beginning on or after July 1, 1999.

(18) Section 32, Article I, and section 1, Article IX of this Constitution, shall not apply to this section.

(19)(a) The Legislative Assembly shall by statute limit the ability of local taxing districts to impose new or additional fees, taxes, assessments or other charges for the purpose of using the proceeds as alternative sources of funding to make up for ad valorem property tax revenue reductions caused by the initial implementation of this section, unless the new or additional fee, tax, assessment or other charge is approved by voters.

(b) This subsection shall not apply to new or additional fees, taxes, assessments or other charges for a government product or service that a person:

(A) May legally obtain from a source other than government; and

(B) Is reasonably able to obtain from a source other than government.

(c) As used in this subsection, "new or additional fees, taxes, assessments or other charges" does not include moneys received by a local taxing district as:

(A) Rent or lease payments;

(B) Interest, dividends, royalties or other investment earnings;

(C) Fines, penalties and unitary assessments;

(D) Amounts charged to and paid by another unit of government for products, services or property; or

(E) Payments derived from a contract entered into by the local taxing district as a proprietary function of the local taxing district.

(d) This subsection does not apply to a local taxing district that derived less than 10 percent of the local taxing district's operating revenues from ad valorem property taxes, other than ad valorem property taxes imposed to pay bonded indebtedness, during the fiscal year ending June 30, 1996.

(e) An election under this subsection need not comply with the voter participation requirements described in subsection (8) of this section.

(20) If any provision of this section is determined to be unconstitutional or otherwise invalid, the remaining provisions shall continue in full force and effect.

Section 11a. School District Tax Levy

Repealed

Section 11b. Property Tax Categories; Limitation on Categories; Exceptions.

(1) During and after the fiscal year 1991-92, taxes imposed upon any property shall be separated into two categories: One which dedicates revenues raised specifically to fund the public school system and one which dedicates revenues raised to fund government operations other than the public school system. The taxes in each category shall be limited as set forth in the table which follows and these limits shall apply whether the taxes imposed on property are calculated on the basis of the value of that property or on some other basis:

MAXIMUM ALLOWABLE TAXES

For Each $1000.00 of Property's Real Market Value

Fiscal Year	School System	Other than Schools
1991-1992	$15.00	$10.00
1992-1993	$12.50	$10.00
1993-1994	$10.00	$10.00
1994-1995	$ 7.50	$10.00
1995-1996	$ 5.00	$10.00

and thereafter

Property tax revenues are deemed to be dedicated to funding the public school system if the revenues are to be used exclusively for educational services, including support services, provided by some unit of government, at any level from pre-kindergarten through post-graduate training.

(2) The following definitions shall apply to this section:

(a) "Real market value" is the minimum amount in cash which could reasonably be expected by an informed seller acting without compulsion, from an informed buyer acting without compulsion, in an "arms-length" transaction during the period for which the property is taxed.

(b) A "tax" is any charge imposed by a governmental unit upon property or upon a property owner as a direct consequence of ownership of that property except incurred charges and assessments for local improvements.

(c) "Incurred charges" include and are specifically limited to those charges by government which can be controlled or avoided by the property owner.

(i) because the charges are based on the quantity of the goods or services used and the owner has direct control over the quantity; or

(ii) because the goods or services are provided only on the specific request of the property owner; or

(iii) because the goods or services are provided by the governmental unit only after the individual property owner has failed to meet routine obligations of ownership and such action is deemed necessary to enforce regulations pertaining to health or safety.

Incurred charges shall not exceed the actual costs of providing the goods or services.

(d) A "local improvement" is a capital construction project undertaken by a governmental unit

(i) which provides a special benefit only to specific properties or rectifies a problem caused by specific properties, and

(ii) the costs of which are assessed against those properties in a single assessment upon the completion of the project, and

(iii) for which the payment of the assessment plus appropriate interest may be spread over a period of at least ten years. The total of all assessments for a local improvement shall not exceed the actual costs incurred by the governmental unit in designing, constructing and financing the project.

(3) The limitations of subsection (1) of this section apply to all taxes imposed on property or property ownership except

(a) Taxes imposed to pay the principal and interest on bonded indebtedness authorized by a specific provision of this Constitution.

(b) Taxes imposed to pay the principal and interest on bonded indebtedness incurred or to be incurred for capital construction or improvements, provided the bonds are offered as general obligations of the issuing governmental unit and provided further that either the bonds were issued not later than November 6, 1990, or the question of the issuance of the specific bonds has been approved by the electors of the issuing governmental unit.

(4) In the event that taxes authorized by any provision of this Constitution to be imposed upon any property should exceed the limitation imposed on either category of taxing units defined in subsection (1) of this section, then, notwithstanding any other provision of this Constitution, the taxes imposed upon such property by the taxing units in that category shall be reduced evenly by the percentage necessary to meet the limitation for that category. The percentages used to reduce the taxes imposed shall be calculated separately for each category and may vary from property to property within the same taxing unit. The limitation imposed by this section shall not affect the tax base of a taxing unit.

(5) The Legislative Assembly shall replace from the State's general fund any revenue lost by the public school system because of the limitations of this section. The Legislative Assembly is authorized, however, to adopt laws which would limit the total of such replacement revenue plus the taxes imposed within the limitations of this section in any year to the corresponding total for the previous year plus 6 percent. This subsection applies only during fiscal years 1991-92 through 1995-96, inclusive.

Section 11c. Limits in Addition to other Tax Limits

The limits in section 11b of this Article are in addition to any limits imposed on individual taxing units by this Constitution.

Section 11d. Effect of Section 11b on Exemptions and Assessments

Nothing in sections 11b to 11e of this Article is intended to require or to prohibit the amendment of any current statute which partially or totally exempts certain classes of property or which prescribes special rules for assessing certain classes of property, unless such amendment is required or prohibited by the implementation of the limitations imposed by section 11b of this Article.

Section 11e. Severability of Sections 11b, 11c and 11d

If any portion, clause or phrase of sections 11b to 11e of this Article is for any reason held to be invalid or unconstitutional by a court of competent jurisdiction, the remaining portions, clauses and phrases shall not be affected but shall remain in full force and effect.

Section 11f. School District Tax Levy Following Merger

Repealed

Section 11g. Tax increase Limitation; Exceptions

Repealed

Section 11h. Voluntary Contributions for Support of Schools or Other Public Entities

Section 11i. Legislation to Implement Limitation and Contribution Provisions

Repealed

Section 11j. Severability of Sections 11g, 11h and 11i

Repealed

Section 11k. Limitation on Applicability of Section 11 (8) Voting Requirements to Elections on Measures Held in May or November of Any Year

Notwithstanding subsection (8) of section 11 of this Article, subsection (8) of section 11 of this Article does not apply to any measure voted on in an election held in May or November of any year.

Section 11L. Limitation on Applicability of Sections 11 and 11b on Bonded Indebtedness to Finance Capital Costs

(1) The limitations of sections 11 and 11b of this Article do not apply to bonded indebtedness incurred by local taxing districts if the bonded indebtedness was incurred on or after January 1, 2011, to finance capital costs as defined in subsection (5) of this section.

(2) Bonded indebtedness described in subsection (1) of this section includes bonded indebtedness issued to refund bonded indebtedness described in subsection (1) of this section.

(3) Notwithstanding subsection (1) of this section, subsection (8) of section 11 of this Article, as limited by section 11k of this Article, applies to measures that authorize bonded indebtedness described in subsection (1) of this section.

(4) The weighted average life of bonded indebtedness incurred on or after January 1, 2011, to finance capital costs may not exceed the weighted average life of the capital costs that are financed with that indebtedness.

(5)(a) As used in this section, "capital costs" means costs of land and of other assets having a useful life of more than one year, including costs associated with acquisition, construction, improvement, remodeling, furnishing, equipping, maintenance or repair.

(b) "Capital costs" does not include costs of routine maintenance or supplies.

Section 12. People's Utility Districts

Peoples' [sic] Utility Districts may be created of territory, contiguous or otherwise, within one or more counties, and may consist of an incorporated municipality, or municipalities, with or without unincorporated territory, for the purpose of supplying water for domestic and municipal purposes; for the development of water power and/or electric energy; and for the distribution, disposal and sale of water, water power and electric energy. Such districts shall be managed by boards of directors, consisting of five members, who shall be residents of such districts. Such districts shall have power:

(a) To call and hold elections within their respective districts.

(b) To levy taxes upon the taxable property of such districts.

(c) To issue, sell and assume evidences of indebtedness.

(d) To enter into contracts.

(e) To exercise the power of eminent domain.

(f) To acquire and hold real and other property necessary or incident to the business of such districts.

(g) To acquire, develop, and/or otherwise provide for a supply of water, water power and electric energy.
Such districts may sell, distribute and/or otherwise dispose of water, water power and electric energy within or without the territory of such districts.

The legislative assembly shall and the people may provide any legislation, that may be necessary, in addition to existing laws, to carry out the provisions of this section.

Section 13. Interests of Employes When Operation of Transportation System Assumed by Public Body

Notwithstanding the provisions of section 20, Article I, section 10, Article VI, and sections 2 and 9, Article XI, of this Constitution, when any city, county, political subdivision, public agency or municipal corporation assumes responsibility for the operation of a public transportation system, the city, county, political subdivision, public agency or municipal corporation shall make fair and equitable arrangements to protect the interests of employes and retired employes affected. Such protective arrangements may include, without being limited to, such provisions as may be necessary for the preservation of rights, privileges and benefits (including continuation of pension rights and payment of benefits) under existing collective bargaining agreements, or otherwise.

Section 14. Metropolitan Service District Charter

(1) The Legislative Assembly shall provide by law a method whereby the legal electors of any metropolitan service district organized under the laws of this state, by majority vote of such electors voting thereon at any legally called election, may adopt, amend, revise or repeal a district charter.
(2) A district charter shall prescribe the organization of the district government and shall provide directly, or by its authority, for the number, election or appointment, qualifications, tenure, compensation, powers and duties of such officers as the district considers necessary. Such officers shall among them exercise all the powers and perform all the duties, as granted to, imposed upon or distributed among district officers by the Constitution or laws of this state, by the district charter or by its authority.

(3) A district charter may provide for the exercise by ordinance of powers granted to the district by the Constitution or laws of this state.

(4) A metropolitan service district shall have jurisdiction over matters of metropolitan concern as set forth in the charter of the district.

(5) The initiative and referendum powers reserved to the people by this Constitution hereby are further reserved to the legal electors of a metropolitan service district relative to the adoption, amendment, revision or repeal of a district charter and district legislation enacted thereunder. Such powers shall be exercised in the manner provided for county measures under section 10, Article VI of this Constitution.

Section 15. Funding of Programs Imposed Upon Local Governments; Exceptions

(1) Except as provided in subsection (7) of this section, when the Legislative Assembly or any state agency requires any local government to establish a new program or provide an increased level of service for an existing program, the State of Oregon shall appropriate and allocate to the local government moneys sufficient to pay the ongoing, usual and reasonable costs of performing the mandated service or activity.

(2) As used in this section:

(a) "Enterprise activity" means a program under which a local government sells products or services in competition with a non-government entity.

(b) "Local government" means a city, county, municipal corporation or municipal utility operated by a board or commission.

(c) "Program" means a program or project imposed by enactment of the Legislative Assembly or by rule or order of a state agency under which a local government must provide administrative, financial, social, health or other specified services to persons, government agencies or to the public generally.

(d) "Usual and reasonable costs" means those costs incurred by the affected local governments for a specific program using generally accepted methods of service delivery and administrative practice.

(3) A local government is not required to comply with any state law or administrative rule or order enacted or adopted after January 1, 1997, that requires the expenditure of money by the local government for a new program or increased level of service for an existing program until the state appropriates and allocates to the local government reimbursement for any costs incurred to carry out the law, rule or order and unless the Legislative Assembly provides, by appropriation, reimbursement in each succeeding year for such costs. However, a local government may refuse to comply with a state law or administrative rule or order under this subsection only if the amount appropriated and allocated to the local government by the Legislative Assembly for a program in a fiscal year:

(a) Is less than 95 percent of the usual and reasonable costs incurred by the local government in conducting the program at the same level of service in the preceding fiscal year; or

(b) Requires the local government to spend for the program, in addition to the amount appropriated and allocated by the Legislative Assembly, an amount that exceeds one-hundredth of one percent of the annual budget adopted by the governing body of the local government for that fiscal year.

(4) When a local government determines that a program is a program for which moneys are required to be appropriated and allocated under subsection (1) of this section, if the local government expended moneys to conduct the program and was not reimbursed under this section for the usual and reasonable costs of the program, the local government may submit the issue of reimbursement to nonbinding arbitration by a panel of three arbitrators. The panel shall consist of one representative from the Oregon Department of Administrative Services, the League of Oregon Cities and the Association of Oregon Counties. The panel shall determine whether the costs incurred by the local government are required to be reimbursed under this section and the amount of reimbursement. The decision of the arbitration panel is not binding upon the parties and may not be enforced by any court in this state.

(5) In any legal proceeding or arbitration proceeding under this section, the local government shall bear the burden of proving by a preponderance of the evidence that moneys appropriated by the Legislative Assembly are not sufficient to reimburse the local government for the usual and reasonable costs of a program.

(6) Except upon approval by three-fifths of the membership of each house of the Legislative Assembly, the Legislative Assembly shall not enact, amend or repeal any law if the anticipated effect of the action is to reduce the amount of state revenues derived from a specific state tax and distributed to local governments as an aggregate during the distribution period for such revenues immediately preceding January 1, 1997.

(7) This section shall not apply to:

(a) Any law that is approved by three-fifths of the membership of each house of the Legislative Assembly.

(b) Any costs resulting from a law creating or changing the definition of a crime or a law establishing sentences for conviction of a crime.

(c) An existing program as enacted by legislation prior to January 1, 1997, except for legislation withdrawing state funds for programs required prior to January 1, 1997, unless the program is made optional.

(d) A new program or an increased level of program services established pursuant to action of the Federal Government so long as the program or increased level of program services imposes costs on local governments that are no greater than the usual and reasonable costs to local governments resulting from compliance with the minimum program standards required under federal law or regulations.

(e) Any requirement imposed by the judicial branch of government.

(f) Legislation enacted or approved by electors in this state under the initiative and referendum powers reserved to the people under section 1, Article IV of this Constitution.

(g) Programs that are intended to inform citizens about the activities of local governments.

(8) When a local government is not required under subsection (3) of this section to comply with a state law or administrative rule or order relating to an enterprise activity, if a non-government entity competes with the local government by selling products or services that are similar to the products and services sold under the enterprise activity, the non-government entity is not required to comply with the state law or administrative rule or order relating to that enterprise activity.

(9) Nothing in this section shall give rise to a claim by a private person against the State of Oregon based on the establishment of a new program or an increased level of service for an existing program without sufficient appropriation and allocation of funds to pay the ongoing, usual and reasonable costs of performing the mandated service or activity.

(10) Subsection (4) of this section does not apply to a local government when the local government is voluntarily providing a program four years after the effective date of the enactment, rule or order that imposed the program.

(11) In lieu of appropriating and allocating funds under this section, the Legislative Assembly may identify and direct the imposition of a fee or charge to be used by a local government to recover the actual cost of the program.

Section 15a. Subsequent Vote for Reaffirmation of Section 15

Repealed

ARTICLE XI-A: FARM AND HOME LOANS TO VETERANS

Section 1. State Empowered to Make Farm and Home Loans to Veterans; Standards and Priorities for Loans

(1) Notwithstanding the limits contained in section 7, Article XI of this Constitution, the credit of the State of Oregon may be loaned and indebtedness incurred in an amount not to exceed eight percent of the true cash value of all the property in the state, for the purpose of creating a fund, to be known as the "Oregon War Veterans' Fund," to be advanced for the acquisition of farms and homes for the benefit of male and female residents of the State of Oregon who served in the Armed Forces of the United States. Secured repayment thereof shall be and is a prerequisite to the advancement of money from such fund, except that moneys in the Oregon War Veterans' Fund may also be appropriated to the Director of Veterans' Affairs to be expended, without security, for the following purposes:

(a) Aiding veterans' organizations in connection with their programs of service to veterans;

(b) Training service officers appointed by the counties to give aid as provided by law to veterans and their dependents;

(c) Aiding the counties in connection with programs of service to veterans;

(d) The duties of the Director of Veterans Affairs as conservator of the estates of beneficiaries of the United States Veterans' Administration; and

(e) The duties of the Director of Veterans Affairs in providing services to veterans, their dependents and survivors.

(2) The Director of Veterans Affairs may establish standards and priorities with respect to the granting of loans from the Oregon War Veterans' Fund that, as determined by the director, best accomplish the purposes and promote the financial sustainability of the Oregon War Veterans' Fund, including, but not limited to, standards and priorities necessary to maintain the tax-exempt status of earnings from bonds issued under authority of this section and section 2 of this Article.

Section 2. Bonds

Bonds of the state of Oregon containing a direct promise on behalf of the state to pay the face value thereof, with the interest therein provided for, may be issued to an amount authorized by section 1 hereof for the purpose of creating said "Oregon War Veterans' Fund." Said bonds shall be a direct obligation of the state and shall be in such form and shall run for such periods of time and bear such rates of interest as provided by statute.

Section 3. Eligibility to Receive Loans.

No person shall receive money from the Oregon War Veterans Fund except the following:

(1) A person who:

(a) Resides in the State of Oregon at the time of applying for a loan from the fund;

(b) Is a veteran, as that term is defined by Oregon law;

(c) Served under honorable conditions on active duty in the Armed Forces of the United States; and

(d) Satisfies the requirements applicable to the funding source for the loan from the Oregon War Veterans Fund.

(2)(a) The spouse of a person who is qualified to receive a loan under subsection (1) of this section but who has either been missing in action or a prisoner of war while on active duty in the Armed Forces of the United States even though the status of missing or being a prisoner occurred prior to completion of a minimum length of service or the person never resided in this state, provided the spouse resides in this state at the time of application for the loan.

(b) The surviving spouse of a person who was qualified to receive a loan under subsection (1) of this section but who died while on active duty in the Armed Forces of the United States even though the death occurred prior to completion of a minimum length of service or the person never resided in this state, provided the surviving spouse resides in this state at the time of application for the loan.

(c) The eligibility of a surviving spouse under this subsection shall terminate on the spouse's remarriage.

(3) As used in this section, "active duty" does not include attendance at a school under military orders, except schooling incident to an active enlistment or a regular tour of duty, or normal military training as a reserve officer or member of an organized reserve or National Guard unit.

Section 4. Tax Levy

There shall be levied each year, at the same time and in the same manner that other taxes are levied, a tax upon all property in the state of Oregon not exempt from taxation, not to exceed two (2) mills on each dollar valuation, to provide for the payment of principal and interest of the bonds authorized to be issued by this article. The two (2) mills additional tax herein provided for hereby is specifically authorized and said tax levy hereby authorized shall be in addition to all other taxes which may be levied according to law.

Section 5. Repeal of Conflicting Constitutional Provisions

The provisions of the constitution in conflict with this amendment hereby are repealed so far as they conflict herewith.

Section 6. Refunding Bonds

Refunding bonds may be issued and sold to refund any bonds issued under authority of sections 1 and 2 of this article. There may be issued and outstanding at any one time bonds aggregating the amount authorized by section 1 hereof, but at no time shall the total of all bonds outstanding, including refunding bonds, exceed the amount so authorized.

ARTICLE XI-B: STATE PAYMENT OF IRRIGATION AND DRAINAGE DISTRICT INTEREST

Repealed

ARTICLE XI-C: WORLD WAR VETERANS STATE AID SINKING FUND

Repealed

ARTICLE XI-D: STATE POWER DEVELOPMENT

Section 1. State's Rights, Title and Interest to Water and Water-Power Sites to be Held in Perpetuity

The rights, title and interest in and to all water for the development of water power and to water power sites, which the state of Oregon now owns or may hereafter acquire, shall be held by it in perpetuity.

Section 2. State's Powers Enumerated

The state of Oregon is authorized and empowered:

1. To control and/or develop the water power within the state;

2. To lease water and water power sites for the development of water power;

3. To control, use, transmit, distribute, sell and/or dispose of electric energy;

4. To develop, separately or in conjunction with the United States, or in conjunction with the political subdivisions of this state, any water power within the state, and to acquire, construct, maintain and/or operate hydroelectric power plants, transmission and distribution lines;

5. To develop, separately or in conjunction with the United States, with any state or states, or political subdivisions thereof, or with any political subdivision of this state, any water power in any interstate stream and to acquire, construct, maintain and/or operate hydroelectric power plants, transmission and distribution lines;

6. To contract with the United States, with any state or states, or political subdivisions thereof, or with any political subdivision of this state, for the purchase or acquisition of water, water power and/or electric energy for use, transmission, distribution, sale and/or disposal thereof;

7. To fix rates and charges for the use of water in the development of water power and for the sale and/or disposal of water power and/or electric energy;

8. To loan the credit of the state, and to incur indebtedness to an amount not exceeding one and one-half percent of the true cash value of all the property in the state taxed on an ad valorem basis, for the purpose of providing funds with which to carry out the provisions of this article, notwithstanding any limitations elsewhere contained in this constitution;

9. To do any and all things necessary or convenient to carry out the provisions of this article.

Section 3. Legislation to Effectuate Article

The legislative assembly shall, and the people may, provide any legislation that may be necessary in addition to existing laws, to carry out the provisions of this article; Provided, that any board or commission created, or empowered to administer the laws enacted to carry out the purposes of this article shall consist of three members and be elected without party affiliation or designation.

Section 4. Construction of Article

Nothing in this article shall be construed to affect in any way the laws, and the administration thereof, now existing or hereafter enacted, relating to the appropriation and use of water for beneficial purposes, other than for the development of water power.

ARTICLE XI-E: STATE REFORESTATION

Section 1. State Empowered to Lend Credit for Forest Rehabilitation and Reforestation; Bonds; Taxation

The credit of the state may be loaned and indebtedness incurred in an amount which shall not exceed at any one time 3/16 of 1 percent of the true cash value of all the property in the state taxed on an ad valorem basis, to provide funds for forest rehabilitation and reforestation and for the acquisition, management, and development of lands for such purposes. So long as any such indebtedness shall remain outstanding, the funds derived from the sale, exchange, or use of said lands, and from the disposal of products therefrom, shall be applied only in the liquidation of such indebtedness. Bonds or other obligations issued pursuant hereto may be renewed or refunded. An ad valorem tax shall be levied annually upon all the property in the state of Oregon taxed on an ad valorem basis, in sufficient amount to provide for the payment of such indebtedness and the interest thereon. The legislative assembly may provide other revenues to supplement or replace the said tax levies. The legislature shall enact legislation to carry out the provisions hereof. This amendment shall supersede all constitutional provisions in conflict herewith.

ARTICLE XI-F(1): HIGHER EDUCATION BUILDING PROJECTS

Section 1. State Empowered to Lend Credit for Higher Education Building Projects

The credit of the state may be loaned and indebtedness incurred in an amount which shall not exceed at any one time three-fourths of one percent of the true cash value of all the taxable property in the state, as determined by law to provide funds with which to acquire, construct, improve, repair, equip and furnish buildings, structures, land and other projects, or parts thereof, that the legislative assembly determines will benefit higher education institutions or activities.

Section 2. Limitation on Authorization to Incur Indebtedness

Indebtedness shall not be incurred to finance projects described in section 1 of this Article unless the constructing authority conservatively estimates that the constructing authority will have sufficient revenues to pay the indebtedness and operate the projects financed with the proceeds of the indebtedness. For purposes of this section, "revenues" includes all funds available to the constructing authority except amounts appropriated by the legislative assembly from the General Fund.

Section 3. Sources of Revenue

Ad valorem taxes shall be levied annually upon all the taxable property in the state of Oregon in sufficient amount, with the aforesaid revenues, to provide for the payment of such indebtedness and the interest thereon. The legislative assembly may provide other revenues to supplement or replace such tax levies.

Section 4. Bonds

Bonds issued pursuant to this article shall be the direct general obligations of the state, and be in such form, run for such periods of time, and bear such rates of interest, as shall be provided by statute. Such bonds may be refunded with bonds of like obligation. Unless provided by statute, no bonds shall be issued pursuant to this article for the construction of buildings or other structures for higher education until after all of the aforesaid outstanding revenue bonds shall have been redeemed or refunded.

Section 5. Legislation to Effectuate Article

The legislative assembly shall enact legislation to carry out the provisions hereof. This article shall supersede all conflicting constitutional provisions.

ARTICLE XI-F(2): VETERANS BONUS

Section 1. State Empowered to Lend Credit to Pay Veterans Bonus; Issuance of Bonds

Notwithstanding the limitations contained in Section 7 of Article XI of the constitution, the credit of the State of Oregon may be loaned and indebtedness incurred to an amount not exceeding 5 percent of the assessed valuation of all the property in the state, for the purpose of creating a fund to be paid to residents of the State of Oregon who served in the armed forces of the United States between September 16, 1940, and June 30, 1946, and were honorably discharged from such service, which fund shall be known as the

"World War II Veterans' Compensation Fund."

Bonds of the State of Oregon, containing a direct promise on behalf of the state to pay the face value thereof with the interest thereon provided for may be issued to an amount authorized in Section 1 hereof for the purpose of creating said World War II Veterans' Compensation Fund. Refunding bonds may be issued and sold to refund any bonds issued under authority of Section 1 hereof. There may be issued and outstanding at any one time bonds aggregating the amount authorized by Section 1, but at no time shall the total of all bonds outstanding, including refunding bonds, exceed the amount so authorized. Said bonds shall be a direct obligation of the State and shall be in such form and shall run for such periods of time and bear such rates of interest as shall be provided by statute. No person shall be eligible to receive money from said fund except the veterans as defined in Section 3 of this act [sic]. The legislature shall and the people may provide any additional legislation that may be necessary, in addition to existing laws, to carry out the provisions of this section.

Section 2. Definitions

The following words, terms, and phrases, as used in this act [sic] shall have the following meaning unless the text otherwise requires:

1. "Domestic service" means service within the continental limits of the United States, excluding Alaska, Hawaii, Canal Zone and Puerto Rico.

2. "Foreign Service" means service in all other places, including sea duty.

3. "Husband" means the unremarried husband, and "wife" means the unremarried wife.

4. "Child or Children" means child or children of issue, child or children by adoption or child or children to whom the deceased person has stood in loco parentis for one year or more immediately preceding his death.

5. "Parent or Parents" means natural parent or parents; parent or parents by adoption; or, person or persons, including stepparent or stepparents, who have stood in loco parentis to the deceased person for a period of one year or more immediately prior to entrance into the armed service of the United States.

6. "Veterans" means any person who shall have served in active duty in the armed forces of the United States at any time between September 16, 1940, and June 30, 1946, both dates inclusive, and who, at the time of commencing such service, was and had been a bona fide resident of the State of Oregon for at least one year immediately preceding the commencement of such service, and who shall have been separated from such service under honorable conditions, or who is still in such service, or who has been retired.

Section 3. Amount of Bonus

Every veteran who was in such service for a period of at least 90 days shall be entitled to receive compensation at the rate of Ten Dollars ($10.00) for each full month during which such veteran was in active domestic service and Fifteen Dollars ($15.00) for each full month during which such veteran was in active foreign service within said period of time. Any veteran who was serving on active duty in the armed forces between September 16, 1940, and June 30, 1946, whose services were terminated by reason of service-connected disabilities, and who, upon filing a claim for disabilities with the United States Veterans Administration within three months after separation from the armed service, was rated not less than 50% disabled as a result of such claim, shall be deemed to have served sufficient time to entitle him or her to the maximum payment under this act [sic] and shall be so entitled. The maximum amount of compensation payable under this act [sic] shall be six hundred dollars ($600.00) and no such compensation shall be paid to any veteran who shall have received from another state a bonus or compensation because of such military service.

Section 4. Survivors of Certain Deceased Veterans Entitled to Maximum Amount

The survivor or survivors, of the deceased veteran whose death was caused or contributed to by a service-connected disease or disability incurred in service under conditions other than dishonorable, shall be entitled, in the order of survivorship provided in this act [sic], to receive the maximum amount of said compensation irrespective of the amount such deceased would have been entitled to receive if living.

Section 5. Certain Persons Not Eligible

No compensation shall be paid under this act [sic] to any veteran who, during the period of service refused on conscientious, political or other grounds to subject himself to full military discipline and unqualified service, or to any veteran for any periods of time spent under penal confinement during the period of active duty, or for service in the merchant marine: Provided, however, that for the purposes of this act [sic], active service in the chaplain corps, or medical corps shall be deemed unqualified service under full military discipline.

Section 6. Order of Distribution Among Survivors

The survivor or survivors of any deceased veteran who would have been entitled to compensation under this act [sic], other than those mentioned in Section 4 of this act [sic], shall be entitled to receive the same amount of compensation as said deceased veteran would have received, if living, which shall be distributed as follows:

1. To the husband or wife, as the case may be, the whole amount.

2. If there be no husband or wife, to the child or children, equally; and

3. If there be no husband or wife or child or children, to the parent or parents, equally.

Section 7. Bonus not Saleable or Assignable; Bonus Free from Creditors Claims and State Taxes

No sale or assignment of any right or claim to compensation under this act [sic] shall be valid, no claims of creditors shall be enforcible against rights or claims to or payments of such compensation, and such compensation shall be exempt from all taxes imposed by the laws of this state.

Section 8. Administration of Article; Rules and Regulations

The director of Veterans' Affairs, State of Oregon, referred to herein as the "director" hereby is authorized and empowered, and it shall be his duty, to administer the provisions of this act [sic], and with the approval of the veterans advisory committee may make such rules and regulations as are deemed necessary to accomplish the purpose hereof.

Section 9. Applications

All applications for certificates under this act [sic] shall be made within two years from the effective date hereof and upon forms to be supplied by the director. Said applications shall be duly verified by the claimant before a notary public or other person authorized to take acknowledgments, and shall set forth applicant's name, residence at the time of entry into the service, date and place of enlistment, induction or entry upon active federal service, beginning and ending dates of foreign service, date of discharge, retirement or release from active federal service, statement of time lost by reason of penal confinement during the period of active duty; together with the applicant's original discharge, or certificate in lieu of lost discharge, or certificate of service, or if the applicant has not been released at the time of application, a statement by competent military authority that the applicant during the period for which compensation is claimed did not refuse to subject himself to full military discipline and unqualified service, and that the applicant has not been separated from service under circumstances other than honorable. The director may require such further information to be included in such application as deemed necessary to enable him to determine the eligibility of the applicant. Such applications, together with satisfactory evidence of honorable service, shall be filed with the director. The director shall make such reasonable requirements for applicants as may be necessary to prevent fraud or the payment of compensation to persons not entitled thereto.

Section 10. Furnishing Forms; Printing, Office Supplies and Equipment; Employees; Payment Of Expenses

The director shall furnish free of charge, upon request, the necessary forms upon which applications may be made and may authorize the county clerks, Veterans organizations and other organizations, and notaries public willing to assist veterans without charge, to act for him in receiving application under this act [sic], and shall furnish such clerks, organizations and notaries public, with the proper forms for such purpose. The director hereby is authorized and directed with the approval of the veterans' advisory committee, to procure such printing, office supplies and equipment and to employ such persons as may be necessary in order to properly carry out the provisions of this act [sic], and all expense incurred by him in the administration thereof shall be paid out of the World War II Veterans Compensation Fund, in the manner provided by law for payment of claims from other state funds.

ARTICLE XI-G: HIGHER EDUCATION INSTITUTIONS AND ACTIVITIES; COMMUNITY COLLEGES

Section 1. State Empowered to Lend Credit for Financing Higher Education Institutions and Activities, and Community Colleges

(1) Notwithstanding the limitations contained in section 7, Article XI of this Constitution, and in addition to other exceptions from the limitations of such section, the credit of the state may be loaned and indebtedness incurred in an amount not to exceed at any time three-fourths of one percent of the true cash value of all taxable property in the state, as determined by law.

(2) Proceeds from any loan authorized or indebtedness incurred under this section shall be used to provide funds with which to acquire, construct, improve, repair, equip and furnish buildings, structures, land and other projects, or parts thereof, that the Legislative Assembly determines will benefit higher education institutions or activities or community colleges authorized by law to receive state aid.

(3) The amount of any indebtedness incurred under this section in any biennium shall be matched by an amount that is at least equal to the amount of the indebtedness. The matching amount must be used for the same or similar purposes as the proceeds of the indebtedness and may consist of moneys appropriated from the General Fund or any other moneys available to the constructing authority for such purposes. However, the matching amount may not consist of proceeds of indebtedness incurred by the state under any other Article of this Constitution. Any matching amount appropriated from the General Fund to meet the requirements of this subsection must be specifically designated therefor by the Legislative Assembly.

(4) Nothing in this section prevents the financing of projects, or parts thereof, by a combination of the moneys available under this section, under Article XI-F(1) of this Constitution, and from other lawful sources.

Section 2. Bonds

Bonds issued pursuant to this Article shall be the direct general obligations of the state and shall be in such form, run for such periods of time, and bear such rates of interest as the Legislative Assembly provides. Such bonds may be refunded with bonds of like obligation.

Section 3. Sources of Revenue

Ad valorem taxes shall be levied annually upon the taxable property within the State of Oregon in sufficient amount to provide for the prompt payment of bonds issued pursuant to this Article and the interest thereon. The Legislative Assembly may provide other revenues to supplement or replace, in whole or in part, such tax levies.

ARTICLE XI-H: POLLUTION CONTROL

Section 1. State Empowered to Lend Credit for Financing Pollution Control Facilities or Related Activities

In the manner provided by law and notwithstanding the limitations contained in sections 7 and 8, Article XI, of this Constitution, the credit of the State of Oregon may be loaned and indebtedness incurred in an amount not to exceed, at any one time, one percent of the true cash value of all taxable property in the state:

(1) To provide funds to be advanced, by contract, grant, loan or otherwise, to any municipal corporation, city, county or agency of the State of Oregon, or combinations thereof, for the purpose of planning, acquisition, construction, alteration or improvement of facilities for or activities related to, the collection, treatment, dilution and disposal of all forms of waste in or upon the air, water and lands of this state; and

(2) To provide funds for the acquisition, by purchase, loan or otherwise, of bonds, notes or other obligations of any municipal corporation, city, county or agency of the State of Oregon, or combinations thereof, issued or made for the purposes of subsection (1) of this section.

Section 2. Only Facilities 70 Percent Self-Supporting and Self-Liquidating Authorized; Exceptions

The facilities for which funds are advanced and for which bonds, notes or other obligations are issued or made and acquired pursuant to this Article shall be only such facilities as conservatively appear to the agency designated by law to make the determination to be not less than 70 percent self-supporting and self-liquidating from revenues, gifts, grants from the Federal Government, user charges, assessments and other fees. This section shall not apply to any activities for which funds are advanced and shall not apply to facilities for the collection, treatment, dilution, removal and disposal of hazardous substances.

Section 3. Authority of Public Bodies to Receive Funds

Notwithstanding the limitations contained in section 10, Article XI of this Constitution, municipal corporations, cities, counties, and agencies of the State of Oregon, or combinations thereof, may receive funds referred to in section 1 of this Article, by contract, grant, loan or otherwise and may also receive such funds through disposition to the state, by sale, loan or otherwise, of bonds, notes or other obligations issued or made for the purposes set forth in section 1 of this Article.

Section 4. Sources of Revenue

Ad valorem taxes shall be levied annually upon all taxable property within the State of Oregon in sufficient amount to provide, together with the revenues, gifts, grants from the Federal Government, user charges, assessments and other fees referred to in section 2 of this Article for the payment of indebtedness incurred by the state and the interest thereon. The Legislative Assembly may provide other revenues to supplement or replace such tax levies.

Section 5. Bonds

Bonds issued pursuant to section 1 of this Article shall be the direct obligations of the state and shall be in such form, run for such periods of time, and bear such rates of interest, as shall be provided by law. Such bonds may be refunded with bonds of like obligation.

Section 6. Legislation to Effectuate Article

The Legislative Assembly shall enact legislation to carry out the provisions of this Article. This Article shall supersede all conflicting constitutional provisions and shall supersede any conflicting provision of a county or city charter or act of incorporation.

ARTICLE XI-I(1): WATER DEVELOPMENT PROJECTS

Section 1. State Empowered to Lend Credit to Establish Water Development Fund; Eligibility; Use

Notwithstanding the limits contained in sections 7 and 8, Article XI of this Constitution, the credit of the State of Oregon may be loaned and indebtedness incurred in an amount not to exceed one and one-half percent of the true cash value of all the property in the state for the purpose of creating a fund to be known as the Water Development Fund. The fund shall be used to provide financing for loans for residents of this state for construction of water development projects for irrigation, drainage, fish protection, watershed restoration and municipal uses and for the acquisition of easements and rights of way for water development projects authorized by law. Secured repayment thereof shall be and is a prerequisite to the advancement of money from such fund. As used in this section, "resident" includes both natural persons and any corporation or cooperative, either for profit or nonprofit, whose principal income is from farming in Oregon or municipal or quasi-municipal or other body subject to the laws of the State of Oregon. Not less than 50 percent of the potential amount available from the fund will be reserved for irrigation and drainage projects. For municipal use, only municipalities and communities with populations less than 30,000 are eligible for loans from the fund.

Section 2. Bonds

Bonds of the State of Oregon containing a direct promise on behalf of the state to pay the face value thereof, with the interest therein provided for, may be issued to an amount authorized by section 1 of this Article for the purpose of creating such fund. The bonds shall be a direct obligation of the state and shall be in such form and shall run for such periods of time and bear such rates of interest as provided by statute.

Section 3. Refunding Bonds

Refunding bonds may be issued and sold to refund any bonds issued under authority of sections 1 and 2 of this Article. There may be issued and outstanding at any time bonds aggregating the amount authorized by section 1 of this Article but at no time shall the total of all bonds outstanding, including refunding bonds, exceed the amount so authorized.

Section 4. Sources of Revenue

Ad valorem taxes shall be levied annually upon all the taxable property in the State of Oregon in sufficient amount to provide for the payment of principal and interest of the bonds issued pursuant to this Article. The Legislative Assembly may provide other revenues to supplement or replace, in whole or in part, such tax levies.

Section 5. Legislation to Effectuate Article

The Legislative Assembly shall enact legislation to carry out the provisions of this Article. This Article supersedes any conflicting provision of a county or city charter or act of incorporation.

ARTICLE XI-I(2): MULTIFAMILY HOUSING FOR ELDERLY AND DISABLED

Section 1. State Empowered to Lend Credit for Multifamily Housing for Elderly and Disabled Persons

In the manner provided by law and notwithstanding the limitations contained in section 7, Article XI of this Constitution, the credit of the State of Oregon may be loaned and indebtedness incurred in an amount not to exceed, at any one time, one-half of one percent of the true cash value of all taxable property in the state to provide funds to be advanced, by contract, grant, loan or otherwise, for the purpose of providing additional financing for multifamily housing for the elderly and for disabled persons. Multifamily housing means a structure or facility designed to contain more than one living unit. Additional financing may be provided to the elderly to purchase ownership interest in the structure or facility.

Section 2. Sources of Revenue

The bonds shall be payable from contract or loan proceeds; bond reserves; other funds available for these purposes; and, if necessary, state ad valorem taxes.

Section 3. Bonds

Bonds issued pursuant to section 1 of this Article shall be the direct obligations of the state and shall be in such form, run for such periods of time and bear such rates of interest as shall be provided by law. The bonds may be refunded with bonds of like obligation.

Section 4. Legislation to effectuate Article

The Legislative Assembly shall enact legislation to carry out the provisions of this Article. This Article shall supersede all conflicting constitutional provisions

ARTICLE XI-J: SMALL SCALE LOCAL ENERGY LOANS

Section 1. State Empowered to Loan Credit for Small Scale Local Energy Loans; Eligibility; Use

Notwithstanding the limits contained in sections 7 and 8, Article XI of this Constitution, the credit of the State of Oregon may be loaned and indebtedness incurred in an amount not to exceed one-half of one percent of the true cash value of all the property in the state for the purpose of creating a fund to be known as the Small Scale Local Energy Project Loan Fund. The fund shall be used to provide financing for the development of small scale local energy projects. Secured repayment thereof shall be and is a prerequisite to the advancement of money from such fund.

Section 2. Bonds

Bonds of the State of Oregon containing a direct promise on behalf of the state to pay the face value thereof, with the interest therein provided for, may be issued to an amount authorized by section 1 of this Article for the purpose of creating such fund. The bonds shall be a direct obligation of the state and shall be in such form and shall run for such periods of time and bear such rates of interest as provided by statute.

Section 3. Refunding Bonds

Refunding bonds may be issued and sold to refund any bonds issued under authority of sections 1 and 2 of this Article. There may be issued and outstanding at any time bonds aggregating the amount authorized by section 1 of this Article but at no time shall the total of all bonds outstanding including refunding bonds, exceed the amount so authorized.

Section 4. Sources of Revenue

Ad valorem taxes shall be levied annually upon all the taxable property in the State of Oregon in sufficient amount to provide for the payment of principal and interest of the bonds issued pursuant to this Article. The Legislative Assembly may provide other revenues to supplement or replace, in whole or in part, such tax levies.

Section 5. Legislation to Effectuate Article

The Legislative Assembly shall enact legislation to carry out the provisions of this Article. This Article supersedes any conflicting provision of a county or city charter or act of incorporation.

ARTICLE XI-K: GUARANTEE OF BONDED INDEBTEDNESS OF EDUCATION DISTRICTS

Section 1. State Empowered to Guarantee Bonded Indebtedness of Education Districts

To secure lower interest costs on the general obligation bonds of school districts, education service districts and community college districts, the State of Oregon may guarantee the general obligation bonded indebtedness of those districts as provided in sections 2 to 6 of this Article and laws enacted pursuant to this Article.

Section 2. State Empowered to Lend Credit for State Guarantee of Bonded Indebtedness of Education Districts

In the manner provided by law and notwithstanding the limitations contained in sections 7 and 8, Article XI of this Constitution, the credit of the State of Oregon may be loaned and indebtedness incurred, in an amount not to exceed, at any one time, one-half of one percent of the true cash value of all taxable property in the state, to provide funds as necessary to satisfy the state guaranty of the bonded general obligation indebtedness of school districts, education service districts and community college districts that qualify, under procedures that shall be established by law, to issue general obligation bonds that are guaranteed by the full faith and credit of this state. The state may guarantee the general obligation debt of qualified school districts, education service districts and community college districts and may guarantee general obligation bonded indebtedness incurred to refund the school district, education service district or community college district general obligation bonded indebtedness.

Section 3. Repayment by Education Districts

The Legislative Assembly may provide that reimbursement to the state shall be obtained from, but shall not be limited to, moneys that otherwise would be used for the support of the educational programs of the school district, the education service district or the community college district that incurred the bonded indebtedness with respect to which any payment under the state's guaranty is made.

Section 4. Sources of Revenue

The State of Oregon may issue bonds if and as necessary to provide funding to satisfy the state's guaranty obligations undertaken pursuant to this Article. In addition, notwithstanding anything to the contrary in Article VIII of this Constitution, the state may borrow available moneys from the Common School Fund if such borrowing is reasonably necessary to satisfy the state's guaranty obligations undertaken pursuant to this Article. The State of Oregon also may issue bonds if and as necessary to provide funding to repay the borrowed moneys, and any interest thereon, to the Common School Fund. The bonds shall be payable from any moneys reimbursed to the state under section 3 of this Article, from any moneys recoverable from the school district, the education service district or the community college district that incurred the bonded indebtedness with respect to which any payment under the state's guaranty is made, any other funds available for these purposes and, if necessary, from state ad valorem taxes.

Section 5. Bonds

Bonds of the state issued pursuant to this Article shall be the direct obligations of the state and shall be in such form, run for such periods of time and bear such rates of interest as shall be provided by law. The bonds may be refunded with bonds of like obligation.

Section 6. Legislation to Effectuate Article

The Legislative Assembly shall enact legislation to carry out the provisions of this Article, including provisions that authorize the state's recovery, from any school district, education service district or community college district that incurred the bonded indebtedness with respect to which any payment under the state's guaranty is made, any amounts necessary to make the state whole. This Article shall supersede all conflicting constitutional provisions and shall supersede any conflicting provision of any law, ordinance or charter pertaining to any school district, education service district or community college district.

ARTICLE XI-L: OREGON HEALTH AND SCIENCE UNIVERSITY

Section 1. State Empowered to Lend Credit for Financing Capital Costs of Oregon Health and Science University; Bonds

(1) In the manner provided by law and notwithstanding the limitations contained in section 7, Article XI of this Constitution, the credit of the State of Oregon may be loaned and indebtedness incurred, in an aggregate outstanding principal amount not to exceed, at any one time, one-half of one percent of the real market value of all property in the state, to provide funds to finance capital costs of Oregon Health and Science University. Bonds issued under this section may not be paid from ad valorem property taxes.

(2) Any indebtedness incurred under this section shall be in the form of general obligation bonds of the State of Oregon containing a direct promise on behalf of the State of Oregon to pay the principal, premium, if any, and interest on such bonds, in an aggregate outstanding principal amount not to exceed the amount authorized in subsection (1) of this section. The bonds shall be the direct obligation of the State of Oregon and shall be in such form, run for such period of time, have such terms and bear such rates of interest as may be provided by statute. The full faith and credit and taxing power of the State of Oregon shall be pledged to the payment of the principal, premium, if any, and interest on such bonds provided, however, that the ad valorem taxing power of the State of Oregon may not be pledged to the payment of such bonds.

(3) The proceeds from bonds issued under this section shall be used to finance capital costs of Oregon Health and Science University and costs of issuing bonds pursuant to this Article. Bonds issued under this section to finance capital costs of Oregon Health and Science University shall be issued in an aggregate principal amount that produces net proceeds for the university in an amount that does not exceed $200 million.

(4) The proceeds from bonds issued under this section may not be used to finance operating costs of Oregon Health and Science University.

(5) As used in this Article, "bonds" means bonds, notes or other financial obligations of the State of Oregon issued under this section

Section 2. Sources of Repayment

The principal, premium, if any, interest and any other amounts payable with respect to bonds issued under section 1 of this Article shall be repaid as determined by the Legislative Assembly from the following sources:

(1) Amounts appropriated for such purpose by the Legislative Assembly from the General Fund, including any taxes levied to pay the bonds other than ad valorem property taxes;

(2) Amounts allocated for such purpose by the Legislative Assembly from the proceeds of the State Lottery or from the Master Settlement Agreement entered into on November 23, 1998, by the State of Oregon and leading United States tobacco product manufacturers; and

(3) Amounts appropriated or allocated for such purpose by the Legislative Assembly from other sources of revenue.

Section 3. Refunding Bonds

Bonds issued under section 1 of this Article may be refunded with bonds of like obligation.

Section 4. Legislation to Effectuate Article

The Legislative Assembly may enact legislation to carry out the provisions of this Article.

Section 5. Relationship to Conflicting Provisions of Constitution

This Article shall supersede all conflicting provisions of this constitution.

ARTICLE XI-M: SEISMIC REHABILITATION OF PUBLIC EDUCATION BUILDINGS

Section 1. State Empowered to Lend Credit for Seismic Rehabilitation of Public Education Buildings; Bonds

(1) In the manner provided by law and notwithstanding the limitations contained in section 7, Article XI of this Constitution, the credit of the State of Oregon may be loaned and indebtedness incurred, in an aggregate outstanding principal amount not to exceed, at any one time, one-fifth of one percent of the real market value of all property in the state, to provide funds for the planning and implementation of seismic rehabilitation of public education buildings, including surveying and conducting engineering evaluations of the need for seismic rehabilitation.

(2) Any indebtedness incurred under this section must be in the form of general obligation bonds of the State of Oregon containing a direct promise on behalf of the State of Oregon to pay the principal, premium, if any, interest and other amounts payable with respect to the bonds, in an aggregate outstanding principal amount not to exceed the amount authorized in subsection (1) of this section. The bonds are the direct obligation of the State of Oregon and must be in a form, run for a period of time, have terms and bear rates of interest as may be provided by statute. The full faith and credit and taxing power of the State of Oregon must be pledged to the payment of the principal, premium, if any, and interest on the general obligation bonds; however, the ad valorem taxing power of the State of Oregon may not be pledged to the payment of the bonds issued under this section.

(3) As used in this section, "public education building" means a building owned by the State Board of Higher Education, a school district, an education service district, a community college district or a community college service district.

Section 2. Sources of Repayment

The principal, premium, if any, interest and other amounts payable with respect to the general obligation bonds issued under section 1 of this Article must be repaid as determined by the Legislative Assembly from the following sources:

(1) Amounts appropriated for the purpose by the Legislative Assembly from the General Fund, including taxes, other than ad valorem property taxes, levied to pay the bonds;

(2) Amounts allocated for the purpose by the Legislative Assembly from the proceeds of the State Lottery or from the Master Settlement Agreement entered into on November 23, 1998, by the State of Oregon and leading United States tobacco product manufacturers; and

(3) Amounts appropriated or allocated for the purpose by the Legislative Assembly from other sources of revenue.

Section 3. Refunding Bonds

General obligation bonds issued under section 1 of this Article may be refunded with bonds of like obligation.

Section 4. Legislation to Effectuate Article

The Legislative Assembly may enact legislation to carry out the provisions of this Article.

Section 5. Relationship to Conflicting Provisions of Constitution

This Article supersedes conflicting provisions of this Constitution.

ARTICLE XI-N: SEISMIC REHABILITATION OF EMERGENCY SERVICES BUILDINGS

Section 1. State Empowered to Lend Credit for Seismic Rehabilitation of Emergency Services Buildings; Bonds

(1) In the manner provided by law and notwithstanding the limitations contained in section 7, Article XI of this Constitution, the credit of the State of Oregon may be loaned and indebtedness incurred, in an aggregate outstanding principal amount not to exceed, at any one time, one-fifth of one percent of the real market value of all property in the state, to provide funds for the planning and implementation of seismic rehabilitation of emergency services buildings, including surveying and conducting engineering evaluations of the need for seismic rehabilitation.

(2) Any indebtedness incurred under this section must be in the form of general obligation bonds of the State of Oregon containing a direct promise on behalf of the State of Oregon to pay the principal, premium, if any, interest and other amounts payable with respect to the bonds, in an aggregate outstanding principal amount not to exceed the amount authorized in subsection (1) of this section. The bonds are the direct obligation of the State of Oregon and must be in a form, run for a period of time, have terms and bear rates of interest as may be provided by statute. The full faith and credit and taxing power of the State of Oregon must be pledged to the payment of the principal, premium, if any, and interest on the general obligation bonds; however, the ad valorem taxing power of the State of Oregon may not be pledged to the payment of the bonds issued under this section.

(3) As used in this section:

(a) "Acute inpatient care facility" means a licensed hospital with an organized medical staff, with permanent facilities that include inpatient beds, and with comprehensive medical services, including physician services and continuous nursing services under the supervision of registered nurses, to provide diagnosis and medical or surgical treatment primarily for but not limited to acutely ill patients and accident victims. "Acute inpatient care facility" includes the Oregon Health and Science University.

(b) "Emergency services building" means a public building used for fire protection services, a hospital building that contains an acute inpatient care facility, a police station, a sheriff's office or a similar facility used by a state, county, district or municipal law enforcement agency.

Section 2. Sources of Repayment

The principal, premium, if any, interest and other amounts payable with respect to the general obligation bonds issued under section 1 of this Article must be repaid as determined by the Legislative Assembly from the following sources:

(1) Amounts appropriated for the purpose by the Legislative Assembly from the General Fund, including taxes, other than ad valorem property taxes, levied to pay the bonds;

(2) Amounts allocated for the purpose by the Legislative Assembly from the proceeds of the State Lottery or from the Master Settlement Agreement entered into on November 23, 1998, by the State of Oregon and leading United States tobacco product manufacturers; and

(3) Amounts appropriated or allocated for the purpose by the Legislative Assembly from other sources of revenue.

Section 3. Refunding Bonds

General obligation bonds issued under section 1 of this Article may be refunded with bonds of like obligation.

Section 4. Legislation to Effectuate Article

The Legislative Assembly may enact legislation to carry out the provisions of this Article.

Section 5. Relationship to Conflicting Provisions of Constitution

This Article supersedes conflicting provisions of this Constitution.

ARTICLE XI-O: PENSION LIABILITIES

Section 1. State Empowered to Lend Credit for Pension Liabilities

(1) In the manner provided by law and notwithstanding the limitations contained in section 7, Article XI of this Constitution, the credit of the State of Oregon may be loaned and indebtedness incurred to finance the State of Oregon's pension liabilities. Indebtedness authorized by this section also may be used to pay costs of issuing or incurring indebtedness under this section.

(2) Indebtedness incurred under this section is a general obligation of the State of Oregon and must contain a direct promise on behalf of the State of Oregon to pay the principal, premium, if any, and interest on that indebtedness. The State of Oregon shall pledge its full faith and credit and taxing power to pay that indebtedness; however, the ad valorem taxing power of the State of Oregon may not be pledged to pay that indebtedness. The amount of indebtedness authorized by this section and outstanding at any time may not exceed one percent of the real market value of all property in the state.

Section 2. Refunding Obligations

Indebtedness incurred under section 1 of this Article may be refunded with like obligations.

Section 3. Legislation to Effectuate Article

The Legislative Assembly may enact legislation to carry out the provisions of this Article.

Section 4. Relationship to Conflicting Provisions of Constitution

This Article supersedes all conflicting provisions of this Constitution.

ARTICLE XI-P: SCHOOL DISTRICT CAPITAL COSTS

Section 1. State Empowered to Lend Credit for Grants or Loans to School Districts to Finance Capital Costs; General Obligation Bond Proceeds as Matching Funds

(1) In the manner provided by law and notwithstanding the limitations contained in section 7, Article XI of this Constitution, the State of Oregon may loan its credit and incur indebtedness, in an aggregate outstanding principal amount not to exceed, at any one time, one-half of one percent of the real market value of the real property in this state, to provide funds to be advanced by grant or loan to school districts to finance the capital costs of the school districts. Bonds issued under this section may not be paid from ad valorem property taxes.

(2) Indebtedness incurred under this section must be in the form of general obligation bonds of the State of Oregon containing a direct promise to pay the principal, interest and premium, if any, of the bonds in an aggregate outstanding principal amount not to exceed the amount authorized in subsection (1) of this section. The bonds are the direct obligation of the State of Oregon and must be in such form, run for such periods of time, have such terms and bear such rates of interest as may be provided by statute. The State of Oregon shall pledge its full faith and credit and taxing power to the payment of the principal, interest and premium, if any, of the bonds. However, the State of Oregon may not pledge its ad valorem taxing power to the payment of the bonds.

(3) The proceeds from bonds issued under this section may be used only to provide matching funds to finance the capital costs of school districts that have received voter approval for local general obligation bonds and to provide for the costs of issuing bonds and the payment of debt service.

(4) The proceeds from bonds issued under this section may not be used to finance the operating costs of school districts.

Section 2. Sources of Repayment

The principal, interest and premium, if any, of the bonds issued under section 1 of this Article must be repaid as determined by the Legislative Assembly from the following sources:

(1) Amounts appropriated for repayment by the Legislative Assembly from the General Fund, including taxes levied to pay the bonds except ad valorem property taxes;

(2) Amounts appropriated or allocated for repayment by the Legislative Assembly from other sources of revenue; or

(3) Any other available moneys.

Section 3. Refunding Bonds

Bonds issued under section 1 of this Article may be refunded with bonds of like obligation.

Section 4. School Capital Matching Fund

(1) There is created a school capital matching fund. Moneys in the fund may be invested and the earnings shall be retained in the fund or expended as provided by the Legislative Assembly.

(2) The Legislative Assembly may by law appropriate, allocate or transfer moneys or revenue to the school capital matching fund.

(3) The Legislative Assembly may appropriate, allocate or transfer moneys in the school capital matching fund and earnings on moneys in the fund for the purposes of providing:

(a) State matching funds to school districts to finance capital costs; and

(b) Payment of debt service for general obligation bonds issued pursuant to this Article.

Section 5. "Capital costs" Defined

As used in this Article, "capital costs" means costs of land and of other assets having a useful life of more than one year, including costs associated with acquisition, construction, improvement, remodeling, furnishing, equipping, maintenance or repair.

Section 6. Legislation to Effectuate Article

The Legislative Assembly may enact legislation to carry out the provisions of this Article.

Section 7. Relationship to Conflicting Provision of Constitution

This Article supersedes any conflicting provision of this Constitution.

ARTICLE XI-Q: REAL OR PERSONAL PROPERTY OWNED OR OPERATED BY STATE

Section 1. State Empowered to Lend Credit for Real or Personal Property to be Owned or Operated by State; Refinancing Authority

(1) In the manner provided by law and notwithstanding the limitations contained in section 7, Article XI of this Constitution, the credit of the State of Oregon may be loaned and indebtedness incurred to finance the costs of:

(a) Acquiring, constructing, remodeling, repairing, equipping or furnishing real or personal property that is or will be owned or operated by the State of Oregon, including, without limitation, facilities and systems;

(b) Infrastructure related to the real or personal property; or

(c) Indebtedness incurred under this subsection.

(2) In the manner provided by law and notwithstanding the limitations contained in section 7, Article XI of this Constitution, the credit of the State of Oregon may be loaned and indebtedness incurred to refinance:

(a) Indebtedness incurred under subsection (1) of this section.

(b) Borrowings issued before the effective date of this Article to finance or refinance costs described in subsection (1) of this section.

Section 2. Limit on Indebtedness; General Obligation of State

(1) Indebtedness may not be incurred under section 1 of this Article if the indebtedness would cause the total principal amount of indebtedness incurred under section 1 of this Article and outstanding to exceed one percent of the real market value of the property in this state.

(2) Indebtedness incurred under section 1 of this Article is a general obligation of the State of Oregon and must contain a direct promise on behalf of the State of Oregon to pay the principal, premium, if any, and interest on the obligation. The full faith and credit and taxing power of the State of Oregon must be pledged to payment of the indebtedness. However, the State of Oregon may not pledge or levy an ad valorem tax to pay the indebtedness.

Section 3. Legislation to Effectuate Article

The Legislative Assembly may enact legislation to carry out the provisions of this Article.

Section 4. Relationship to Conflicting Provisions of Constitution

This Article supersedes conflicting provisions of this Constitution.

ARTICLE XII: STATE PRINTING

Section 1. State printing; State Printer

Laws may be enacted providing for the state printing and binding, and for the election or appointment of a state printer, who shall have had not less than ten years' experience in the art of printing. The state printer shall receive such compensation as may from time to time be provided by law. Until such laws shall be enacted the state printer shall be elected, and the printing done as heretofore provided by this constitution and the general laws.

ARTICLE XIII: SALARIES

Repealed

ARTICLE XIV: SEAT OF GOVERNMENT

Section 1. Seat of Government

The permanent seat of government for the state shall be Marion County.

Section 2. Erection of State House Prior to 1865

No tax shall be levied, or money of the State expended, or debt contracted for the erection of a State House prior to the year eighteen hundred and sixty five.

ARTICLE XV: MISCELLANEOUS

Section 1. Officers to Hold Office Until Successors Elected; Exceptions; Effect on Defeated Incumbent

(1) All officers, except members of the Legislative Assembly and incumbents who seek reelection and are defeated, shall hold their offices until their successors are elected, and qualified.

(2) If an incumbent seeks reelection and is defeated, he shall hold office only until the end of his term; and if an election contest is pending in the courts regarding that office when the term of such an incumbent ends and a successor to the office has not been elected or if elected, has not qualified because of such election contest, the person appointed to fill the vacancy thus created shall serve only until the contest and any appeal is finally determined notwithstanding any other provision of this constitution.

Section 2. Tenure of office; how fixed; maximum tenure. When the duration of any office is not provided for by this Constitution, it may be declared by law; and if not so declared, such office shall be held during the pleasure of the authority making the appointment. But the Legislative Assembly shall not create any office, the tenure of which shall be longer than four years.

Section 3. Oaths of office. Every person elected or appointed to any office under this Constitution, shall, before entering on the duties thereof, take an oath or affirmation to support the Constitution of the United States, and of this State, and also an oath of office.

Note: The amendments to sections 4, 4a, 4b and 4c and the repeal of section 4d by Measure No. 76, 2010, as submitted to the people were preceded by a preamble that reads as follows:

PREAMBLE: The people of the State of Oregon find that renewing the current dedication in the Oregon Constitution of fifteen percent of lottery revenues to parks, water quality and fish and wildlife habitats will provide lasting social, economic, environmental and public health benefits.

The people of the State of Oregon also find that renewal of the Parks and Natural Resources Fund will support voluntary efforts to:

(1) Protect and restore water quality, watersheds and habitats for native fish and wildlife that provide a healthy environment for current and future generations of Oregonians;

(2) Maintain and expand public parks, natural areas and recreation areas to meet the diverse needs of a growing population and to provide opportunities for [sic] to experience nature and enjoy outdoor recreation activities close to home and in the many special places throughout Oregon;

(3) Provide jobs and economic opportunities improving the health of our forests, prairies, lakes, streams, wetlands, rivers, and parks, including efforts to halt the spread of invasive species;

(4) Strengthen the audit and reporting requirements, identify desired outcomes and specify allowable uses of the fund in order to provide more strategic, accountable and efficient uses of the Parks and Natural Resources Fund; and

(5) Enhance the ability of public land managers, private organizations, individuals and businesses to work together in local, regional and statewide partnerships to expand recreation opportunities, improve water quality and conserve fish and wildlife habitat.

Section 4. Regulation of Lotteries; State Lottery; Use of Net Proceeds from State Lottery

(1) Except as provided in subsections (2), (3), (4), (8) and (9) of this section, lotteries and the sale of lottery tickets, for any purpose whatever, are prohibited, and the Legislative Assembly shall prevent the same by penal laws.

(2) The Legislative Assembly may provide for the establishment, operation, and regulation of raffles and the lottery commonly known as bingo or lotto by charitable, fraternal, or religious organizations. As used in this section, charitable, fraternal or religious organization means such organizations or foundations as defined by law because of their charitable, fraternal, or religious purposes. The regulations shall define eligible organizations or foundations, and may prescribe the frequency of raffles, bingo or lotto, set a maximum monetary limit for prizes and require a statement of the odds on winning a prize. The Legislative Assembly shall vest the regulatory authority in any appropriate state agency.

(3) There is hereby created the State Lottery Commission which shall establish and operate a State Lottery. All proceeds from the State Lottery, including interest, but excluding costs of administration and payment of prizes, shall be used for any of the following purposes: creating jobs, furthering economic development, financing public education in Oregon or restoring and protecting Oregon's parks, beaches, watersheds and native fish and wildlife.

(4)(a) The State Lottery Commission shall be comprised of five members appointed by the Governor and confirmed by the Senate who shall serve at the pleasure of the Governor. At least one of the Commissioners shall have a minimum of five years experience in law enforcement and at least one of the Commissioners shall be a certified public accountant. The Commission is empowered to promulgate rules related to the procedures of the Commission and the operation of the State

Lottery. Such rules and any statutes enacted to further implement this article shall insure the integrity, security, honesty, and fairness of the Lottery. The Commission shall have such additional powers and duties as may be provided by law.

(b) The Governor shall appoint a Director subject to confirmation by the Senate who shall serve at the pleasure of the Governor. The Director shall be qualified by training and experience to direct the operations of a state-operated lottery. The Director shall be responsible for managing the affairs of the Commission. The Director may appoint and prescribe the duties of no more than four Assistant Directors as the Director deems necessary. One of the Assistant Directors shall be responsible for a security division to assure security, integrity, honesty, and fairness in the operations and administration of the State Lottery. To fulfill these responsibilities, the Assistant Director for security shall be qualified by training and experience, including at least five years of law enforcement experience, and knowledge and experience in computer security.

(c) The Director shall implement and operate a State Lottery pursuant to the rules, and under the guidance, of the Commission. The State Lottery may operate any game procedure authorized by the commission, except parimutuel racing, social games, and the games commonly known in Oregon as bingo or lotto, whereby prizes are distributed using any existing or future methods among adult persons who have paid for tickets or shares in that game; provided that, in lottery games utilizing computer terminals or other devices, no coins or currency shall ever be dispensed directly to players from such computer terminals or devices.

(d) There is hereby created within the General Fund the Oregon State Lottery Fund which is continuously appropriated for the purpose of administering and operating the Commission and the State Lottery. The State Lottery shall operate as a self-supporting revenue-raising agency of state government and no appropriations, loans, or other transfers of state funds shall be made to it. The State Lottery shall pay all prizes and all of its expenses out of the revenues it receives from the sale of tickets or shares to the public and turnover the net proceeds therefrom to a fund to be established by the Legislative Assembly from which the Legislative Assembly shall make appropriations for the benefit of any of the following public purposes: creating jobs, furthering economic development, financing public education in Oregon or restoring and protecting Oregon's parks, beaches, watersheds and native fish and wildlife. Effective July 1, 1997, 15% of the net proceeds from the State Lottery shall be deposited, from the fund created by the Legislative Assembly under this paragraph, in an education stability fund. Effective July 1, 2003, 18% of the net proceeds from the State Lottery shall be deposited, from the fund created by the Legislative Assembly under this paragraph, in an education stability fund. Earnings on moneys in the education stability fund shall be retained in the fund or expended for the public purpose of financing public education in Oregon as provided by law. Except as provided in subsection (6) of this section, moneys in the education stability fund shall be invested as provided by law and shall not be subject to the limitations of section 6, Article XI of this Constitution. The Legislative Assembly may appropriate other moneys or revenue to the education stability fund. The Legislative Assembly shall appropriate amounts sufficient to pay lottery bonds before appropriating the net proceeds from the State Lottery for any other purpose. At least 84% of the total annual revenues from the sale of all lottery tickets or shares shall be returned to the public in the form of prizes and net revenues benefiting the public purpose.

(5) Notwithstanding paragraph (d) of subsection (4) of this section, the amount in the education stability fund created under paragraph (d) of subsection (4) of this section may not exceed an amount that is equal to five percent of the amount that was accrued as revenues in the state's General Fund during the prior biennium. If the amount in the education stability fund exceeds five percent of the amount that was accrued as revenues in the state's General Fund during the prior biennium:

(a) Additional net proceeds from the State Lottery may not be deposited in the education stability fund until the amount in the education stability fund is reduced to less than five percent of the amount that was accrued as revenues in the state's General Fund during the prior biennium; and

(b) Fifteen percent of the net proceeds from the State Lottery shall be deposited into the school capital matching fund created under section 4, Article XI-P of this Constitution.

(6) The Legislative Assembly may by law appropriate, allocate or transfer any portion of the principal of the education stability fund created under paragraph (d) of subsection (4) of this section for expenditure on public education if:

(a) The proposed appropriation, allocation or transfer is approved by three-fifths of the members serving in each house of the Legislative Assembly and the Legislative Assembly finds one of the following:

(A) That the last quarterly economic and revenue forecast for a biennium indicates that moneys available to the state's General Fund for the next biennium will be at least three percent less than appropriations from the state's General Fund for the current biennium;

(B) That there has been a decline for two or more consecutive quarters in the last 12 months in seasonally adjusted nonfarm payroll employment; or

(C) That a quarterly economic and revenue forecast projects that revenues in the state's General Fund in the current biennium will be at least two percent below what the revenues were projected to be in the revenue forecast on which the legislatively adopted budget for the current biennium was based; or

(b) The proposed appropriation, allocation or transfer is approved by three-fifths of the members serving in each house of the Legislative Assembly and the Governor declares an emergency.

(7) The Legislative Assembly may by law prescribe the procedures to be used and identify the persons required to make the forecasts described in subsection (6) of this section.

(8) Effective July 1, 1999, 15% of the net proceeds from the State Lottery shall be deposited in a parks and natural resources fund created by the Legislative Assembly. Of the moneys in the parks and natural resources fund, 50% shall be deposited in a parks sub-account and distributed for the public purposes of financing the protection, repair, operation, and creation of state, regional and local public parks, ocean shore and public beach access areas, historic sites and recreation areas, and 50% shall be deposited in a natural resources sub-account and distributed for the public purposes of financing the restoration and protection of native fish and wildlife, watersheds and water quality in Oregon. The Legislative Assembly shall not limit expenditures from the parks and natural resources fund, or from the parks or natural resources sub-accounts. The Legislative Assembly may appropriate other moneys or revenue to the parks and natural resources fund.

(9) Only one State Lottery operation shall be permitted in the State.

(10) The Legislative Assembly has no power to authorize, and shall prohibit, casinos from operation in the State of Oregon.

Section 4a. Use of Net Proceeds from State Lottery for Parks and Recreation Areas

(1) In each biennium the Legislative Assembly shall appropriate all of the moneys in the parks sub-account of the parks and natural resources fund established under section 4 of this Article for the uses allowed in subsection (2) of this section, and to achieve all of the following:

(a) Provide additional public parks, natural areas or outdoor recreational areas to meet the needs of current and future residents of the State of Oregon;

(b) Protect natural, cultural, historic and outdoor recreational resources of state or regional significance;

(c) Manage public parks, natural areas and outdoor recreation areas to ensure their long-term ecological health and provide for the enjoyment of current and future residents of the State of Oregon; and

(d) Provide diverse and equitable opportunities for residents of the State of Oregon to experience nature and participate in outdoor recreational activities in state, regional, local or neighborhood public parks and recreation areas.

(2) The moneys in the parks sub-account shall be used only to:

(a) Maintain, construct, improve, develop, manage and operate state parks, ocean shores, public beach access areas, historic sites, natural areas and outdoor and recreation areas;

(b) Acquire real property, or interests therein, that has significant natural, scenic, cultural, historic or recreational values, for the creation or operation of state parks, ocean shores, public beach access areas, outdoor recreation areas and historic sites; and

(c) Provide grants to regional or local government entities to acquire property for public parks, natural areas or outdoor recreation areas, or to develop or improve public parks, natural areas or outdoor recreation areas.

(3) In each biennium the Legislative Assembly shall appropriate no less than twelve percent of the moneys in the parks sub-account for local and regional grants as authorized under paragraph (c) of subsection (2) of this section. However, if in any biennium the amount of net proceeds deposited in the parks and natural resources fund created under section 4 of this Article increases by more than fifty percent above the amount deposited in the 2009-2011 biennium, the Legislative Assembly shall appropriate no less than twenty-five percent of the moneys in the parks sub-account for local and regional grants as authorized under paragraph (c) of subsection (2) of this section. The grants shall be administered by a single state agency. The costs of the state agency in administering the grants shall not be paid out of the portion of the moneys in the parks sub-account appropriated for local and regional grants.

Section 4b. Use of Net Proceeds from State Lottery for Fish and Wildlife, Watershed and Habitat Protection

(1) In each biennium the Legislative Assembly shall appropriate all of the moneys in the natural resources sub-account of the parks and natural resources fund established under section 4 of this Article for the uses allowed in subsections (2) and (3) of this section, and to accomplish all of the following:

(a) Protect and improve water quality in Oregon's rivers, lakes, and streams by restoring natural watershed functions or stream flows;

(b) Secure long-term protection for lands and waters that provide significant habitats for native fish and wildlife;

(c) Restore and maintain habitats needed to sustain healthy and resilient populations of native fish and wildlife;

(d) Maintain the diversity of Oregon's plants, animals and ecosystems;

(e) Involve people in voluntary actions to protect, restore and maintain the ecological health of Oregon's lands and waters; and

(f) Remedy the conditions that limit the health of fish and wildlife, habitats and watershed functions in greatest need of conservation.

(2) In each biennium the Legislative Assembly shall appropriate no less than sixty-five percent of the moneys in the natural resources sub-account to one state agency, and that agency shall distribute those moneys as grants to entities other than state or federal agencies for projects that achieve the outcomes specified in subsection (1) of this section. However, if in any biennium the amount of net proceeds deposited in the parks and natural resources fund created under section 4 of this Article increases by more than fifty percent above the amount deposited in the 2009-2011 biennium, the Legislative Assembly shall appropriate no less than seventy percent of the moneys in the natural resources sub-account to one state agency, and that agency shall distribute those moneys as grants to entities other than state or federal agencies for projects that achieve the outcomes specified in subsection (1) of this section. In addition, these moneys shall be used only to:

(a) Acquire from willing owners interests in land or water that will protect or restore native fish or wildlife habitats, which interests may include but are not limited to fee interests, conservation easements or leases;

(b) Carry out projects to protect or restore native fish or wildlife habitats;

(c) Carry out projects to protect or restore natural watershed functions to improve water quality or stream flows; and

(d) Carry out resource assessment, planning, design and engineering, technical assistance, monitoring and outreach activities necessary for projects funded under paragraphs (a) through (c) of this subsection.

(3) In each biennium the Legislative Assembly shall appropriate that portion of the natural resources subaccount not appropriated under subsection (2) of this section to support all of the following activities:

(a) Develop, implement or update state conservation strategies or plans to protect or restore native fish or wildlife habitats or to protect or restore natural watershed functions to improve water quality or stream flows;

(b) Develop, implement or update regional or local strategies or plans that are consistent with the state strategies or plans described in paragraph (a) of this subsection;

(c) Develop, implement or update state strategies or plans to prevent, detect, control or eradicate invasive species that threaten native fish or wildlife habitats or that impair water quality;

(d) Support local delivery of programs or projects, including watershed education activities, that protect or restore native fish or wildlife habitats or watersheds;

(e) Pay the state agency costs of administering subsection (2) of this section, which costs shall not be paid out of the moneys available for grants under subsection (2) of this section; and

(f) Enforce fish and wildlife and habitat protection laws and regulations.

Section 4c. Audit of Agency Receiving Certain net Proceeds from State Lottery

The Secretary of State shall regularly audit any state agency that receives moneys from the parks and natural resources fund established under section 4 of this Article to address the financial integrity, compliance with applicable laws, efficiency and effectiveness of the use of the moneys. The costs of the audit shall be paid from the parks and natural resources fund. However, such costs may not be paid from the portions of such fund, or the sub-accounts of the fund, that are dedicated to grants. The audit shall be submitted to the Legislative Assembly as part of a biennial report to the Legislative Assembly. In addition, each agency that receives moneys from the parks and natural resources fund shall submit a biennial performance report [sic] the Legislature [sic] Assembly that describes the measurable biennial and cumulative results of activities and programs financed by the fund.

Section 4d. Subsequent Vote for Reaffirmation of Sections 4a, 4b and 4c and Amendment to Section 4

Repealed

Section 4e. Transfer of Moneys in School Capital Matching Sub-Account to School Capital Matching Fund Created Under Section 4, Article XI-P

Repealed

Section 4f. Percentage of Lottery Revenues to be Expended for Benefit of Veterans

(1) Effective July 1, 2017, 1.5 percent of the net proceeds from the State Lottery shall be deposited, from the fund created by the Legislative Assembly under paragraph (d) of subsection (4) of section 4 of this Article, in a veterans' services fund created by the Legislative Assembly. The Legislative Assembly may appropriate other moneys or revenue to the veterans' services fund.

(2) The moneys in the veterans' services fund may be used only to provide services for the benefit of veterans. Such services may include, without limitation:

(a) Assistance for veterans with reintegration, employment, education benefits and tuition, housing, physical and mental health care and addiction treatment programs;

(b) Assistance for veterans, spouses of veterans or dependents of veterans in accessing state and federal benefits; and

(c) Funding services provided by county veterans' service officers, campus veterans' service officers or nonprofit or tribal veterans' service officers.

(3) As used in this section, "veteran" means a resident of the State of Oregon who served in the Armed Forces of the United States.

Section 5. Property of Married Women not Subject to Debts of Husband; Registration of Separate Property

The property and pecuniary rights of every married woman, at the time of marriage or afterwards, acquired by gift, devise, or inheritance shall not be subject to the debts, or contracts of the husband; and laws shall be passed providing for the registration of the wife's seperate [sic] property.

Section 5a. Policy Regarding Marriage

It is the policy of Oregon, and its political subdivisions, that only a marriage between one man and one woman shall be valid or legally recognized as a marriage.

Section 6. Minimum Area and Population of Counties

No county shall be reduced to an area of less than four hundred square miles; nor shall any new county be established in this State containing a less area, nor unless such new county shall contain a population of at least twelve hundred inhabitants.

Section 7. Officers Not to Receive Fees From or Represent Claimants Against State

No State officers, or members of the Legislative Assembly, shall directly or indirectly receive a fee, or be engaged as counsel, agent, or Attorney in the prosecution of any claim against this State.

Section 8. Certain Persons Not To Hold Real Estate or Mining Claims; Working Mining Claims

Repealed

Section 8. Persons Eligible to Serve in Legislature; Employment of Judges by Oregon National Guard or Public University.

Notwithstanding the provisions of section 1, Article III and section 10, Article II of this Constitution:

(1) A person employed by any board or commission established by law to supervise and coordinate the activities of Oregon's institutions of post-secondary education, a person employed by a public university as defined by law or a member or employee of any school board is eligible to serve as a member of the Legislative Assembly, and membership in the Legislative Assembly does not prevent the person from being employed by any board or commission established by law to supervise and coordinate the activities of Oregon's post-secondary institutions of education or by a public university as defined by law, or from being a member or employee of a school board.

(2) A person serving as a judge of any court of this state may be employed by the Oregon National Guard for the purpose of performing military service or may be employed by any public university as defined by law for the purpose of teaching, and the employment does not prevent the person from serving as a judge.

Section 8a. Repealed

Section 9. When Elective Office Becomes Vacant

The Legislative Assembly may provide that any elective public office becomes vacant, under such conditions or circumstances as the Legislative Assembly may specify, whenever a person holding the office is elected to another public office more than 90 days prior to the expiration of the term of the office he is holding. For the purposes of this section, a person elected is considered to be elected as of the date the election is held.

Section 10. The Oregon Property Protection Act of 2000

(1) This section may be known and shall be cited as the "Oregon Property Protection Act of 2000."

(2) Statement of principles. The People, in the exercise of the power reserved to them under the Constitution of the State of Oregon, declare that:

(a) A basic tenet of a democratic society is that a person is presumed innocent and should not be punished until proven guilty;

(b) The property of a person generally should not be forfeited in a forfeiture proceeding by government unless and until that person is convicted of a crime involving the property;

(c) The value of property forfeited should be proportional to the specific conduct for which the owner of the property has been convicted; and

(d) Proceeds from forfeited property should be used for treatment of drug abuse unless otherwise specified by law for another purpose.

(3) Forfeitures prohibited without conviction. Except as provided in this section, a judgment of forfeiture of property in a civil forfeiture proceeding by the State or any of its political subdivisions may not be entered until and unless the person claiming the property is convicted of a crime in Oregon or another jurisdiction and the property:

(a) Constitutes proceeds of the crime for which the claimant has been convicted;

(b) Was instrumental in committing or facilitating the crime for which the claimant has been convicted;

(c) Constitutes proceeds of one or more other crimes similar to the crime for which the claimant was convicted; or

(d) Was instrumental in committing or facilitating one or more other crimes similar to the crime for which the claimant was convicted.

(4) Forfeiture based on similar crimes. Property may be forfeited under paragraph (c) or (d) of subsection (3) of this section only if the claimant is notified in writing of the other crime or crimes claimed to be similar to the crime for which the claimant was convicted. The notice must be given at the time the claimant is given notice of the seizure of the property for forfeiture, and the claimant must have an opportunity to challenge the seizure and forfeiture of the property.

(5) Forfeiture without conviction of claimant. The property of a claimant who has not been convicted of a crime may be forfeited in a civil forfeiture proceeding only if the claimant consents to the forfeiture of the property or the forfeiting agency proves the property constitutes proceeds or an instrumentality of crime committed by another person as described in subsection (3) of this section and:

(a) The claimant took the property with the intent to defeat forfeiture of the property;

(b) The claimant knew or should have known that the property constituted proceeds or an instrumentality of criminal conduct; or

(c) The claimant acquiesced in the criminal conduct. A person shall be considered to have acquiesced in criminal conduct if the person knew of the criminal conduct and failed to take reasonable action under the circumstances to terminate the criminal conduct or prevent use of the property to commit or facilitate the criminal conduct.

(6) Standard of proof. (a) Except as provided in paragraph (b) of this subsection, if the property to be forfeited in a civil forfeiture action is personal property, the forfeiting agency must prove the elements specified in subsection (3) or (5) of this section by a preponderance of the evidence. If the property to be forfeited in a civil forfeiture action is real property, the forfeiting agency must prove the elements specified in subsection (3) or (5) of this section by clear and convincing evidence.

(b) If a forfeiting agency establishes in a forfeiture proceeding that cash, weapons or negotiable instruments were found in close proximity to controlled substances or to instrumentalities of criminal conduct, the burden is on any person claiming the cash, weapons or negotiable instruments to prove by a preponderance of the evidence that the cash, weapons or negotiable instruments are not proceeds of criminal conduct or an instrumentality of criminal conduct.

(7) Value of property forfeited. The value of the property forfeited under the provisions of this section may not be excessive and shall be substantially proportional to the specific conduct for which the owner of the property has been convicted. For purposes of this section, "property" means any interest in anything of value, including the whole of any lot or tract of land and tangible and intangible personal property, including currency, instruments or securities or any other kind of privilege, interest, claim or right whether due or to become due. Nothing in this section shall prohibit a person from voluntarily giving a judgment of forfeiture.

(8) Financial institutions. In a civil forfeiture proceeding, if a financial institution claiming an interest in the property demonstrates that it holds an interest, the financial institution's interest is not subject to forfeiture.

(9) Exception for unclaimed property and contraband. Notwithstanding the provisions of subsection (3) of this section, if, following notice to all persons known to have an interest or who may have an interest, no person claims an interest in the seized property or if the property is contraband, a judgment of forfeiture may be allowed and entered without a criminal conviction. For purposes of this subsection, "contraband" means personal property, articles or things, including but not limited to controlled substances or drug paraphernalia, that a person is prohibited by Oregon statute or local ordinance from producing, obtaining or possessing.

(10) Exception for forfeiture of animals. This section does not apply to the forfeiture of animals that have been abused, neglected or abandoned.

(11) Law enforcement seizures unaffected. Nothing in this section shall be construed to affect the temporary seizure of property for evidentiary, forfeiture, or protective purposes, or to alter the power of the Governor to remit fines or forfeitures under Article V, Section 14, of this Constitution.

(12) Disposition of property to drug treatment. Any sale of forfeited property shall be conducted in a commercially reasonable manner. Property forfeited in a civil forfeiture proceeding shall be distributed or applied in the following order:

(a) To the satisfaction of any foreclosed liens, security interests and contracts in the order of their priority;

(b) To the State or any of its political subdivisions for actual and reasonable expenses related to the costs of the forfeiture proceeding, including attorney fees, storage, maintenance, management, and disposition of the property incurred in connection with the sale of any forfeited property; and

(c) To the State or any of its political subdivisions to be used exclusively for drug treatment, unless another disposition is specially provided by law.

(13) Restrictions on State transfers. Neither the State of Oregon, its political subdivisions, nor any forfeiting agency shall transfer forfeiture proceedings to the federal government unless a state court has affirmatively found that:

(a) The activity giving rise to the forfeiture is interstate in nature and sufficiently complex to justify the transfer;

(b) The seized property may only be forfeited under federal law; or

(c) Pursuing forfeiture under state law would unduly burden the state forfeiting agencies.

(14) Penalty for violations. Any person acting under color of law, official title or position who takes any action intending to conceal, transfer, withhold, retain, divert or otherwise prevent any moneys, conveyances, real property, or any things of value forfeited under the law of this State or the United States from being applied, deposited or used in accordance with the requirements of this section shall be subject to a civil penalty in an amount treble the value of the forfeited property concealed, transferred, withheld, retained or diverted. Nothing in this subsection shall be construed to impair judicial immunity if otherwise applicable.

(15) Reporting requirement. All forfeiting agencies shall report the nature and disposition of all property seized for forfeiture or forfeited to a State asset forfeiture oversight committee that is independent of any forfeiting agency. The asset forfeiture oversight committee shall generate and make available to the public an annual report of the information collected. The asset forfeiture oversight committee shall also make recommendations to ensure that asset forfeiture proceedings are handled in a manner that is fair to innocent property owners and interest holders.

(16) Severability. If any part of this section or its application to any person or circumstance is held to be invalid for any reason, then the remaining parts or applications to any persons or circumstances shall not be affected but shall remain in full force and effect.

Note: The text of section 11 (sections 1 to 3, Measure No. 99, 2000) as submitted to the people was preceded by a preamble that reads as follows:

WHEREAS, thousands of Oregon seniors and persons with disabilities live independently in their own homes, which they prefer and is less costly than institutional care (i.e. nursing homes), because over 10,000 home care workers, (also known as client employed providers), paid by the State of Oregon provide in-home support services;

WHEREAS, home care workers provide services that range from housekeeping, shopping, meal preparation, money management and personal care to medical care and treatment, but receive little, if any, training in those areas resulting in a detrimental impact on quality of care;

WHEREAS, the quality of care provided to seniors and people with disabilities is diminished when there is a lack of stability in the workforce which is the result of home care workers receiving low wages, minimal training and benefits;

WHEREAS, both home care workers and clients receiving home care services would benefit from creating an entity which has the authority to provide, and is held accountable for the quality of services provided in Oregon's in-home system of long-term care.

Section 11. Home Care Commission

(1) Ensuring High Quality Home Care Services: Creation and Duties of the Quality Home Care Commission. (a) The Home Care Commission is created as an independent public commission consisting of nine members appointed by the Governor.

(b) The duties and functions of the Home Care Commission include, but are not limited to:

(A) Ensuring that high quality, comprehensive home care services are provided to the elderly and people with disabilities who receive personal care services in their homes by home care workers hired directly by the client and financed by payments from the State or by payments from a county or other public agency which receives money for that purpose from the State;

(B) Providing routine, emergency and respite referrals of qualified home care providers to the elderly and people with disabilities who receive personal care services by home care workers hired directly by the client and financed in whole or in part by the State, or by payment from a county or other public agency which receives money for that purpose from the State;

(C) Provide training opportunities for home care workers, seniors and people with disabilities as consumers of personal care services;

(D) Establish qualifications for home care workers;

(E) Establish and maintain a registry of qualified home care workers;

(F) Cooperate with area agencies on aging and disability services and other local agencies to provide the services described and set forth in this section.

(2) Home Care Commission Operation/Selection. (a) The Home Care Commission shall be comprised of nine members. Five members of the Commission shall be current or former consumers of home care services for the elderly or people with disabilities. One member shall be a representative of the Oregon Disabilities Commission, (or a successor entity, for as long as a comparable entity exists). One member shall be a representative of the Governor's Commission on Senior Services, (or a successor entity, for as long as a comparable entity exists). One member shall be a representative of the Oregon Association of Area Agencies on Aging and Disabilities, (or a successor entity, for as long as a comparable entity exists). One member shall be a representative of the Senior and Disabled Services Division, (or a successor entity, for as long as a comparable entity exists).

(b) The term of office of each member is three years, subject to confirmation by the Senate. If there is a vacancy for any cause, the Governor shall make an appointment to become immediately effective for the unexpired term. A member is eligible for reappointment and may serve no more than three consecutive terms. In making appointments to the Commission, the Governor may take into consideration any nominations or recommendations made by the representative groups or agencies.

(3) Other Provisions — Legal Duties and Responsibilities of the Commission

(a) The Home Care Commission shall, in its own name, for the purpose of carrying into effect and promoting its functions, have authority to contract, lease, acquire, hold, own, encumber, insure, sell, replace, deal in and with and dispose of real and personal property.

(b) When conducting any activities in this Section or in subsection (1) of this section, and in making decisions relating to those activities, the Home Care Commission shall first consider the effect of its activities and its decisions on improving the quality of service delivery and ensuring adequate hours of service are provided to clients who are served by home care workers.

(c) Clients of home care services retain their right to select the providers of their choice, including family members.

(d) Employees of the Commission are not employees of the State of Oregon for any purpose.

(e) Notwithstanding the provisions in paragraph (d) of this subsection, the State of Oregon shall be held responsible for unemployment insurance payments for home care workers.

(f) For purposes of collective bargaining, the Commission shall be the employer of record of home care workers hired directly by the client and paid by the State, or by a county or other public agency which receives money for that purpose from the State. Home care workers have the right to form, join and participate in the activities of labor organizations of their own choosing for the purpose of representation and collective bargaining with the Commission on matters concerning employment relations. These rights shall be exercised in accordance with the rights granted to public employees with mediation and interest arbitration as the method of concluding the collective bargaining process. Home care workers shall not have the right to strike.

(g) The Commission may adopt rules to carry out its functions.

ARTICLE XVI: BOUNDARIES

Section 1. State Boundaries

The State of Oregon shall be bounded as provided by section 1 of the Act of Congress of February 1859, admitting the State of Oregon into the Union of the United States, until:

(1) Such boundaries are modified by appropriate interstate compact or compacts heretofore or hereafter approved by the Congress of the United States; or

(2) The Legislative Assembly by law extends the boundaries or jurisdiction of this state an additional distance seaward under authority of a law heretofore or hereafter enacted by the Congress of the United States.

ARTICLE XVII: AMENDMENTS AND REVISIONS

Section 1. Method of Amending Constitution

Any amendment or amendments to this Constitution may be proposed in either branch of the legislative assembly, and if the same shall be agreed to by a majority of all the members elected to each of the two houses, such proposed amendment or amendments shall, with the yeas and nays thereon, be entered in their journals and referred by the secretary of state to the people for their approval or rejection, at the next regular general election, except when the legislative assembly shall order a special election for that purpose. If a majority of the electors voting on any such amendment shall vote in favor thereof, it shall thereby become a part of this Constitution. The votes for and against such amendment, or amendments, severally, whether proposed by the legislative assembly or by initiative petition, shall be canvassed by the secretary of state in the presence of the governor, and if it shall appear to the governor that the majority of the votes cast at said election on said amendment, or amendments, severally, are cast in favor thereof, it shall be his duty forthwith after such canvass, by his proclamation, to declare the said amendment, or amendments, severally, having received said majority of votes to have been adopted by the people of Oregon as part of the Constitution thereof, and the same shall be in effect as a part of the Constitution from the date of such proclamation. When two or more amendments shall be submitted in the manner aforesaid to the voters of this state at the same election, they shall be so submitted that each amendment shall be voted on separately. No convention shall be called to amend or propose amendments to this Constitution, or to propose a new Constitution, unless the law providing for such convention shall first be approved by the people on a referendum vote at a regular general election. This article shall not be construed to impair the right of the people to amend this Constitution by vote upon an initiative petition therefor.

Section 2. Method of Revising Constitution

(1) In addition to the power to amend this Constitution granted by section 1, Article IV, and section 1 of this Article, a revision of all or part of this Constitution may be proposed in either house of the Legislative Assembly and, if the proposed revision is agreed to by at least two-thirds of all the members of each house, the proposed revision shall, with the yeas and nays thereon, be entered in their journals and referred by the Secretary of State to the people for their approval or rejection, notwithstanding section 1, Article IV of this Constitution, at the next regular state-wide primary election, except when the Legislative Assembly orders a special election for that purpose. A proposed revision may deal with more than one subject and shall be voted upon as one question. The votes for and against the proposed revision shall be canvassed by the Secretary of State in the presence of the Governor and, if it appears to the Governor that the majority of the votes cast in the election on the proposed revision are in favor of the proposed revision, he shall, promptly following the canvass, declare, by his proclamation, that the proposed revision has received a majority of votes and has been adopted by the people as the Constitution of the State of Oregon or as a part of the Constitution of the State of Oregon, as the case may be. The revision shall be in effect as the Constitution or as a part of this Constitution from the date of such proclamation.

(2) Subject to subsection (3) of this section, an amendment proposed to the Constitution under section 1, Article IV, or under section 1 of this Article may be submitted to the people in the form of alternative provisions so that one provision will become a part of the Constitution if a proposed revision is adopted by the people and the other provision will become a part of the Constitution if a proposed revision is rejected by the people. A proposed amendment submitted in the form of alternative provisions as authorized by this subsection shall be voted upon as one question.

(3) Subsection (2) of this section applies only when:

(a) The Legislative Assembly proposes and refers to the people a revision under subsection (1) of this section; and

(b) An amendment is proposed under section 1, Article IV, or under section 1 of this Article; and

(c) The proposed amendment will be submitted to the people at an election held during the period between the adjournment of the legislative session at which the proposed revision is referred to the people and the next regular legislative session.

ARTICLE XVIII: SCHEDULE

Section 1. Election to Accept or Reject Constitution

For the purpose of taking the vote of the electors of the State, for the acceptance or rejection of this Constitution, an election shall be held on the second Monday of November, in the year 1857, to be conducted according to existing laws regulating the election of Delegates in Congress, so far as applicable, except as herein otherwise provided.

Section 2. Questions Submitted to Voters

Each elector who offers to vote upon this Constitution, shall be asked by the judges of election this question:

Do you vote for the Constitution? Yes, or No.

And also this question:

Do you vote for Slavery in Oregon? Yes, or No.

And in the poll books shall be columns headed respectively.

"Constitution, Yes."

"Constitution, No"

"Slavery, Yes."

"Slavery, No".

And the names of the electors shall be entered in the poll books, together with their answers to the said questions, under their appropriate heads. The abstracts of the votes transmitted to the Secretary of the Territory, shall be publicly opened, and canvassed by the Governor and Secretary, or by either of them in the absence of the other; and the Governor, or in his absence the

Secretary, shall forthwith issue his proclamation, and publish the same in the several newspapers printed in this State, declaring the result of the said election upon each of said questions.

Section 3. Majority of Votes Required to Accept or Reject Constitution

If a majority of all the votes given for, and against the Constitution, shall be given for the Constitution, then this Constitution shall be deemed to be approved, and accepted by the electors of the State, and shall take effect accordingly; and if a majority of such votes shall be given against the Constitution, then this Constitution shall be deemed to be rejected by the electors of the State, and shall be void.

Section 4. Vote on Certain Sections of Constitution

If this Constitution shall be accepted by the electors, and a majority of all the votes given for, and against slavery, shall be given for slavery, then the following section shall be added to the Bill of Rights, and shall be part of this Constitution:

"Sec. ___"Persons lawfully held as slaves in any State, Territory, or District of the United States, under the laws thereof, may be brought into this State, and such Slaves, and their descendants may be held as slaves within this State, and shall not be emancipated without the consent of their owners."

And if a majority of such votes shall be given against slavery, then the foregoing section shall not, but the following sections shall be added to the Bill of Rights, and shall be a part of this Constitution.

"Sec. ___There shall be neither slavery, nor involuntary servitude in the State, otherwise than as a punishment for crime, whereof the party shall have been duly convicted."

Section 5. Apportionment of Senators and Representatives

Until an enumeration of the inhabitants of the State shall be made, and the senators and representatives apportioned as directed in the Constitution, the

County of Marion shall have two senators, and four representatives.

Linn two senators, and four representatives.

Lane two senators, and three representatives.

Clackamas and Wasco, one senator jointly, and Clackamas three representatives, and Wasco one representative.

Yamhill one senator, and two representatives.

Polk one senator, and two representatives.

Benton one senator, and two representatives.

Multnomah, one senator, and two representatives.

Washington, Columbia, Clatsop, and Tillamook one senator jointly, and Washington one representative, and Washington and Columbia one representative jointly, and Clatsop and Tillamook one representative jointly.

Douglas, one senator, and two representatives.

Jackson one senator, and three representatives.

Josephine one senator, and one representative.

Umpqua, Coos and Curry, one senator jointly, and Umpqua one representative, and Coos and Curry one representative jointly.

Section 6. Election Under Constitution; Organization of State

If this Constitution shall be ratified, an election shall be held on the first Monday of June 1858, for the election of members of the Legislative Assembly, a Representative in Congress, and State and County officers, and the Legislative Assembly shall convene at the Capital on the first Monday of July 1858, and proceed to elect two senators in Congress, and make such further provision as may be necessary to the complete organization of a State government.

Section 7. Former Laws Continued in Force

All laws in force in the Territory of Oregon when this Constitution takes effect, and consistent therewith, shall continue in force until altered, or repealed.

Section 8. Officers to Continue in Office

All officers of the Territory of Oregon, or under its laws, when this Constitution takes effect, shall continue in office, until superseded by the State authorities.

Section 9. Crimes Against Territory

Crimes and misdemeanors committed against the Territory of Oregon shall be punished by the State, as they might have been punished by the Territory, if the change of government had not been made.

Section 10. Saving Existing Rights and Liabilities

All property and rights of the Territory, and of the several counties, subdivisions, and political bodies corporate, of, or in the Territory, including fines, penalties, forfeitures, debts and claims, of whatsoever nature, and recognizances, obligations, and undertakings to, or for the use of the Territory, or any county, political corporation, office, or otherwise, to or for the public, shall inure to the State, or remain to the county, local division, corporation, officer, or public, as if the change of government had not been made. And private rights shall not be affected by such change.

Section 11. Judicial Districts

Until otherwise provided by law, the judicial districts of the State, shall be constituted as follows:

The counties of Jackson, Josephine, and Douglas, shall constitute the first district.

The counties of Umpqua, Coos, Curry, Lane, and Benton, shall constitute the second district.

The counties of Linn, Marion, Polk, Yamhill and Washington, shall constitute the third district.

The counties of Clackamas, Multnomah, Wasco, Columbia, Clatsop, and Tillamook, shall constitute the fourth district

The County of Tillamook shall be attached to the county of Clatsop for judicial purposes.